Focused Assessment

Enriching the Instructional Cycle

GWEN DOTY

Solution Tree | Press

a division of

Solution Tree

555 North Morton Street
Bloomington, IN 47404
800.733.6786 (toll free) / 812.336.7700
FAX: 812.336.7790

email: info@solution-tree.com
solution-tree.com

Printed in the United States of America

11 10 09   3 4 5

FSC
Mixed Sources
Product group from well-managed
forests and other controlled sources
Cert no. SW-COC-002283
www.fsc.org
© 1996 Forest Stewardship Council

ISBN 978-1-935249-66-5

Teaching in Focus
A Solution Tree Series

This series by Gwen Doty, building on the success of the differentiated instructional model, offers practical advice on how to respond to the needs and learning style of every student in the classroom in an increasingly standards-driven environment. The books cover such topics as scaffolding and customizing the learning, unpacking the language of the standards, maintaining the dynamic between assessment and instruction, and nourishing in students a deep and ongoing love for thinking and learning.

Also in this series:

Focused Instruction: An Innovative Teaching Model for All Learners
Words First: Learning the Language of the Standards
Not Just for the Test: Learning That Lasts
Creating Lifelong Learners: Nourishing the Independent Mind

The reproducible tools in this book and links to the websites mentioned can be found online at teachinginfocus.com.

Gwen Doty

Gwen Doty delivers seminars nationwide, emphasizing customized strategies based on student readiness. The creator of numerous accredited graduate courses for educators and the codeveloper of an online instructional database, Gwen has acquired a depth of experience in many areas—as a teacher, an administrator, and a professional development specialist. She holds an advanced degree in oral communications, and throughout her career she has trained teachers and parents in the best ways to communicate with students. An independent consultant, Gwen has long advocated the integration of emotional and social components in academic lessons. When not writing and speaking, she raises alpacas with her husband in Chino Valley, Arizona.

Dedication

With love and gratitude to Duane Doty: my husband, best friend, and ever-patient sounding board.

Acknowledgments

Because each and every day I learn something new and significant about the world of education, I could never thank all those who have provided me with their wisdom and insight regarding best practices. Here I will attempt to acknowledge just a few of these people.

This book would never have been written if I had not had opportunities to visit numerous classrooms throughout the country and to observe the educational practices of many dedicated teachers and administrators. So, first and foremost, I'd like to express my admiration and gratitude to those professionals who work endlessly to improve student performance. Bravo to your commitment to education!

My colleagues and employers throughout my years as teacher, principal, and professional consultant have all had an impact on my current views regarding high-quality instructional and assessment practices. This list of advisors includes Dr. Sandra Darling, B. J. Pavlich, Cassandra Erkens, Claudia Wheatley, Dr. Jan Elsea, my mother, who was a teacher for over 30 years, and my father, who was a superintendent of schools.

My husband, Duane Doty, and my editor, Ed Levy, have been ever-patient with my writing endeavors and always willing to listen and advise when I needed it. Many thanks for your support and encouragement! Last but not least, my thanks also go to Raven Bongiani, who worked tirelessly on the design of the text.

Table of Contents

Introduction

Focused Assessment: Enriching the Instructional Cycle uses a research-based design that promotes an ongoing "check for understanding" throughout the learning process. The focused assessment model teaches the use of purposeful and relevant assessment, from preassessment to the completion of a final student product. It involves students in the process of gaining a clear understanding of their skill and knowledge proficiency and takes into account different learning styles, so that students may demonstrate evidence of competence in ways that make sense to them. Lastly, focused assessment is a consistent reflection of content standards—the objectives that were actually taught—and student data.

Focused Assessment involves a systematic process that embraces the concept of "assessment for learning." It provides customizations that enable all learners to demonstrate proficiency according to their readiness level.

Why Should We "Focus Our Assessments"?

The primary reason to assess student learning should be to *improve* student learning and teacher effectiveness. Thus, as we will keep emphasizing, assessment must be an ongoing process used throughout the learning cycle. It should be a purposeful and natural process that happens in conjunction with instruction, one that focuses attention on the refinements or revisions needed in the instruction. Let's take a look at how focused assessment works in Lisa Schmidtgall's seventh-grade classroom.

Lisa Schmidtgall's Seventh-Grade Math Class

Lisa Schmidtgall walks around the classroom with a checklist in hand while observing students working in collaborative groups. In their science class, these students are currently studying the effects of water shortages on communities and they are gathering statistics, which also offers them opportunity to use some of the problem-solving techniques they are learning in math. Four problem-solving strategies are listed on the board to remind students of their options as they seek answers to the water-shortage dilemma. As Lisa moves from group to group, she asks questions and listens for appropriate use of problem-solving techniques and strategies. On her checklist, she records a "+" next to the names of students who demonstrate one or more effective problem-solving methods that she has taught. Next to those who demonstrate a partial understanding, she records a "P." Next to the names of those who show little or no understanding of effective problem-solving techniques, she records a "–". At the end of the period, Lisa asks students to write at least two paragraphs in their math journals to explain the techniques they have used to solve math problems related to the local water shortage. The combination of hearing an oral demonstration and reading a written response gives her a comprehensive picture of which students need additional instruction and which students are ready to broaden their learning.

What Do We Want Our Assessments to Tell Us?

Depending on the institution or entity that is involved, the specific kind of questions that need to be answered through assessment vary:

State Level

- How well are our schools doing around the state?
- Which schools are excelling, and what are the causes for their success?
- How do different districts conduct assessments throughout the school year?

School and District Level

- How are we doing in specific areas?
- In what areas could our students improve overall?
- What kinds of assessments are successful teachers employing throughout the year?

Classroom Level

- How can I assess accurately, without spending more hours?
- How well are my students mastering the content standards?
- In which areas are individual students falling short of proficiency?
- In which areas are a high percentage of students having problems?
- How can I use student assessment to better design my instruction?

Student Level

- How well did I understand the content?
- In which areas do I need to improve?
- Which assessment format makes the most sense to me?
- How do I best show what I know?

Assessments need to flow naturally from classroom instruction and involve activities that make sense to students. However, given the realities of our educational system, students must also learn skills for taking selected-response assessments, to prepare themselves for standardized testing.

Before creating or implementing a focused assessment, it is also helpful to answer the following questions:

- What knowledge or skills are students expected to achieve, and to what degree should they learn them? This is usually determined through an analysis of the state standards. Both teacher and student need a clear understanding of the learning target.

- What are the performance criteria—the guidelines, rules, and attributes—that will be used to judge the quality of student performance?

- Why is the assessment taking place? Both teacher and student should have a clear understanding of the purposes behind it—for example, the need to gather information about how well individual students understand a portion or benchmark of a lesson or unit, or what students know prior to the content instruction. Or it may be to determine how well students understand essential knowledge before you convey more advanced concepts.

- Based on your purpose for assessing, which format (such as multiple choice, essay, portfolio, presentation) should you use?

After creating the assessment, ensure that it reflects the content standards or goals being taught and that the performance criteria are stated clearly, excluding irrelevant features of performance. (For example, if your goal is to assure student knowledge of the Civil War and you choose an essay format, you would exclude writing standards, such as punctuation, from the performance criteria.)

How Can Focused Assessment Become a Natural Part of the Instructional Process?

As the standards-based movement continues to gain momentum and we hold students responsible for high academic standards, we must develop assessment methods that accurately measure, interpret, and communicate what students know—and the depth to which they know it. Using a variety of measurements instead of one or two to make this determination will give you a much more focused idea of how effective you have been in teaching the standards, as well as how effective your students were in meeting the goals. To see how this works, let's compare two classrooms.

Scenario 1: Mr. Jamison's Sixth-Grade Math Class

Mr. Jamison teaches sixth-grade mathematics at Littlepoint Middle School. In teaching a unit on measurement, he used direct instruction, followed by an assignment out of the math book. Each day, as students entered the classroom, he asked them to take out their math assignments and exchange papers, and then they orally graded the papers. Mr. Jamison would then ask students to let him know which problem was the most difficult, and they would work it out on the board and discuss it. At the end of the measurement unit, Mr. Jamison gave a final assessment to determine how well his students understood the important concepts from the unit.

Scenario 2: Ms. Gonzales' Eighth-Grade Math Class

Ms. Gonzales, who teaches eighth-grade math at Rockview Middle School, took a very different approach. She divided her unit on measurement into four natural segments: 1) geometric properties and attributes, 2) the transformation of shapes, 3) spatial relationships using coordinate geometry, and 4) units and techniques of measurement. In addition to receiving daily direct instruction, students used math journals to record their understanding at the end of each day. After reading the journal entries and looking at student work, Ms. Gonzales worked with small groups of students who had similar skill levels. At the end of each of the measurement segments, she gave the students a small project to complete to demonstrate their understanding of the segment's goals. When all four of the measurement segments were fully explored and Ms. Gonzales felt most students were confident, she asked each of them to create a project board to display all of their segment mini projects, as well as their final journal entry, which detailed their understanding of each of the four segments. The project board served as a final compilation of the many activities they had created throughout the learning experience.

*   *   *

Because Ms. Gonzales provided multiple opportunities to assess student learning throughout the unit and because these opportunities were varied (learning journals met the needs of verbal-linguistic learners, while projects met the needs of visual and kinesthetic learners), she was able to acquire a focused picture of what her students know and how well they know it. And because she assessed student understanding throughout the unit, she was able to stop and reteach or change her pacing as needed.

Throughout the unit, she could also determine in which areas a large percentage of students performing poorly required her to reteach the goals using a different instructional strategy. For areas in which only a few students performed poorly, Ms. Gonzales had the option of grouping them together to reteach.

Mr. Jamison, on the other hand, acquired very little knowledge of how well his students understood the content, other than what he learned from the final test. With his assessment style, students either sink or swim. Unfortunately, assessment in

Mr. Jamison's classroom was *not* a natural component of the instructional process but rather something tacked onto the end of a unit. He also learned very little about what he did that was effective. The only informed decision Mr. Jamison can now make is whether to move on to the next unit or reteach the entire class.

To be valuable, assessment must be viewed as a natural component that occurs in every lesson on every day of instruction. It can be as simple as observing students as they discuss their understandings or as complex as a student music performance or multiple-choice quiz. Whatever form it takes, an effective focused assessment should have these characteristics:

1. It should be ongoing and coincide with instruction.

2. It must be varied, so that students with different learning styles have opportunities to demonstrate their understanding in ways that make sense to them.

3. It should appropriately reflect the content standards and the information that was actually taught.

The cycle of planning, instructing, learning, and assessing is continuous and ever-evolving, with the overall goal of answering these two vital questions for teachers: *How effective was my teaching, and how proficient are my learners?* Knowing the answers to these questions leads to better teaching methods and techniques, new versions of assessment, and new avenues for gaining awareness of student proficiency.

The Spectrum of Formats

Think of focused assessment as any purposeful activity that provides information to be used as feedback for modifying teaching and learning. In a typical lesson or unit, you might give a preassessment prior to the lesson, keep an observation checklist during it, and assign an essay, presentation, or project at the end. The assessment could also take the form of a writing exercise consisting of stages, such as prewriting, rough-draft writing, revised writing, and final draft writing.

Summative assessments occur at the end of the lesson and may take on any form, from performance-based to selected-response formats. Their purpose is specifically to measure student success, and if they are used as the only assessment, they cannot be used to inform teachers and students throughout the learning cycle. Table I-1 compares formative and summative assessment and gives examples of typical formats for each.

Table I-1. Comparing Formative and Summative Assessment

TYPE OF ASSESSMENT	FORMAT
Formative Assessment Ongoing, varied, a tool for learning and diagnosing	Performance assessments: Essay, journal, presentation, report, diorama, poster, and so on. Selected response: Multiple choice, true/false, fill in the blank, matching
Summative Assessment A single test, usually given at the end of a lesson, unit, or semester, to measure achievement	Selected response (most likely format): Multiple choice, true false, fill in the blank, matching Performance assessments: Essay, journal, presentation, report, diorama, poster, and so on

What Are the Steps That Lead to Focused Assessment?

The subsequent chapters of this book share with you the essential steps for creating effective, focused assessments for your specific classroom, standards and goals, content discipline, student learning styles, and diversities. In the first six chapters, you will learn the fine points of the six focused-assessment components, and in the seventh you will learn how to launch your own unit and reflect on the results. The six components are as follows:

1. Value the continuous learning cycle.

2. Lay the groundwork for assessment.

3. Work from learning targets to assessments.

4. Choose from a variety of assessment formats.

5. Customize the chosen assessment format.

6. Create a unit assessment plan.

At the end of every chapter, you will find reproducible tools and resources to use in preparing your assessments. These tools are also available online on the website for the Teaching in Focus series, teachinginfocus.com.

Valuing the Continuous Learning Cycle

Just as a finished architectural blueprint must contain everything needed to guide the actual construction of a building (including plumbing, electrical, door-and-window scheme, and so on), it is necessary to first design the "big picture" blueprint of a comprehensive instruction and assessment model.

—Larry B. Ainsworth and Donald J. Viegut

In this chapter . . .

- Thinking About Assessment
- A Continuous Cycle of Teaching and Assessing
- Student Involvement in Assessment
- The Language of Assessment
- Thinking About Your Thinking
- Tools and Templates

Thinking About Assessment

Reflect upon the types of assessment that your students are often asked to complete. Which of them are scored and graded, and which are used to simply inform? How often do you assess your students throughout a lesson? What formats do you use? Do all your students receive the same assessment?

A Continuous Cycle of Teaching and Assessing

The continuous learning cycle may help to answer some of the above questions. We have broken the continuous learning cycle into the following four components.

As you can see, the first three are generally considered to be formative assessment (assessments that "inform" instruction; the last is summative, or "final," in that it contributes to the grade).

1. Preassessment

2. Informal assessment

3. Growth assessment

4. Final student product

Let's look at each of these components individually.

Preassessment

A preassessment determines what students already know as you begin instruction on a new skill. Used diagnostically, it informs both you and the student about the student's current level of understanding.

Never record the scores from preassessments in a grade book, as this tool is meant only to inform and guide your instructional practices. Examples of preassessment formats include whole-class discussions with teacher questions, graphic organizers, journal entries, and multiple-choice formats.

Based on the preassessment results as well as your observation and prior knowledge, you may then choose to "layer" the learning—as well as any future assessments—based on student need. Techniques for layering are discussed in detail in volume one of the Teaching in Focus series, *Focused Instruction*. In brief, there are three instructional layers:

1. The *essential knowledge* layer, in which students are expected to know the basic or general concepts of the target

2. The *application* layer, in which students know the concepts and can utilize them

3. The *complex-thinking* layer, in which students know the concepts and can also apply them in higher-order thinking situations

Informal Assessment

Informal assessments should occur in conjunction with all stages of learning. During direct instruction, you can stop every few minutes to assess how well students are learning. You might say, "Now turn to a partner and explain this concept in your own words." As students are talking to their partners, walk around listening for their level of understanding. Informal assessments like these give you valuable information and answer the following questions:

- Do I need to reteach this content?

- Do I need to approach this differently or try another teaching strategy that might make more sense to students?

- Do I need to work with a small group of students who need additional teaching?

- How should I inform students of their progress or specific areas needing improvement?

Informal assessment can also occur as students work on a practice assignment following a lesson. At this point, don't expect them to have mastered the content or process, but as they practice, assess their progress. Often these assessments are as simple as walking around the classroom with a checklist in hand or sitting next to a student and saying, "Tell me how you arrived at this answer."

Informal assessments can also take the form of student self-reflections. As students complete an initial lesson, ask them to share their new learning or their current understanding of the concept. Also ask them to share what was easy and what was difficult. Again, because students have not yet had adequate practice with feedback, do not use informal assessments in grading.

Growth Assessment

Growth assessments measure degrees of learning as students gain more skill and higher levels of understanding. What distinguishes them from informal assessments is the expectation for the learning: Students are now expected to have some skill and knowledge regarding the learning target. Examples of growth assessments include essays, mini-presentations, kinesthetic activities, and selected-response assessments. Growth assessments often involve performance tasks that use a rubric for scoring.

As you move through the process, you have repeated opportunities to focus and refocus your assessments, that is, to adjust and customize them according to your students' readiness levels. This doesn't mean that some students are less accountable for learning the standard than any other; but some will need additional teaching, practice, and feedback before you expect them to become proficient to the degree that the standard is requiring.

Final Student Product

The final student product is the big finale and demonstrates the depth of student understanding of the goal. However, don't mistake "final" as meaning "done" with the teaching or learning. In the continuous learning model, the learning continues. The final product can be an accumulation of prior learning tasks, a project, oral presentation, research paper, or demonstration. Although you will likely be converting student scores into grades, the final product still informs you and the student about what is needed next. Questions such as the following may arise:

- Do I still need to reteach parts of the content to certain students?

- Will I need to revisit these concepts with students periodically in order to enhance retention of information?

- Will this learning enhance or be a preview for future learning?

Using these four stages of formative assessment ensures that students and teachers are continually apprised regarding levels of academic proficiency. A general guideline is to use the preassessment and all informal assessments to inform and provide specific feedback to students and to use growth assessments and the final student product scores as a real measurement of student proficiency with the learning target. When you design assessment so that it truly flows naturally from instruction and student investigations, it isn't difficult to motivate students. Often they will not view the assessment task as an assessment at all, but simply as a learning activity. That is the epitome of effective assessment—when goals, instruction, activities, and assessment are viewed as one continuous learning cycle.

Figure 1-1 shows the continuous learning cycle for a unit that a teacher is monitoring and evaluating using formative assessment.

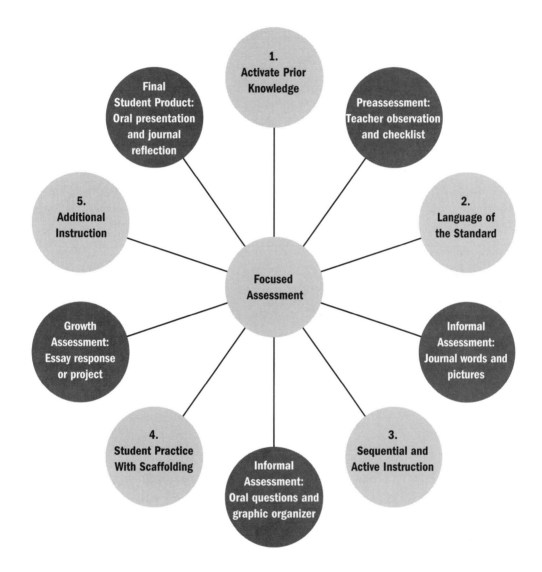

Figure 1-1. The Continuous Learning Cycle

You could substitute any number of formats for the examples shown in the figure.

Student Involvement in Assessment

A very important aspect of assessment that we must address in this first chapter is student involvement. Keeping students motivated to learn, engaged in the process, and on task at all times is a monumental job. When students feel that they have no ownership in the process or that they are the audience rather than the participants, they will not be inspired or take responsibility for the learning. Black and Wiliam (1998) found that when attempting to motivate students during the learning process, emphasizing grades is not a strong motivator and, in fact, can actually impede student success. Rather, students respond well to specific teacher feedback.

Very early on in the lesson, communicate to students that not only are they expected to learn, but they also have some options regarding how they will demonstrate their knowledge. Rather than keeping your instructional goals a secret that students need to guess, view your students as partners in the process. Clearly articulating the learning targets and posting them in the classroom will help students stay focused. Sharing a rubric or list of criteria in advance of the lesson is another way to ensure they are included. There may be times when students help design the criteria for the rubric. Throughout the learning cycle, from preassessment through final student product, encourage your students to compare their work to the criteria of the rubric, so that the target comes into focus for them. Revisit the goals regularly. Having multiple opportunities to measure their work against the criteria allows students to determine their own strengths and weaknesses and to better understand how to improve their performance. Provide students with an ongoing self-assessment sheet, like the one in Table 1-1, to keep a record of their growth.

Students should use the self-assessment chart throughout the focused assessment learning cycle of preassessment, informal assessment, growth assessment, and final student product. In the example given, after students draw a rough-draft map of their home for the preassessment, the teacher sees which map skills they need the most help with. Throughout the informal assessment and growth assessment phase of the learning, students continuously improve their maps. In its final form, the map becomes the final student product.

Table 1-1. Student Self-Assessment Sheet

Performance Task:			
Create a map showing the inside of your home. Write a paragraph that explains your map.			

Performance Criteria:
The map clearly shows all of the rooms, hallways, closets, and other parts of the house.
The map has a title and key. Symbols in the map match the key.
The map is clearly marked and labeled, easy to read, and colorful.
A written paragraph clearly explains the map, key, symbols, and labels.

Date:	In comparing my work to the criteria, these are my strengths:	In comparing my work to the criteria, these are my weaknesses:	Here are my next steps toward reaching the targets:

Giving timely and specific feedback at regular intervals also helps to keep students involved and motivated. When students are regularly told about the areas in which they are progressing well and ways to improve in the places they aren't, they see a clear direction to move toward. Give both formal and informal feedback. Formal feed-back includes student-teacher conferences in which both of you view and discuss the student's work. It also includes specific written feedback. Informal feedback may be a dialogue between student and teacher or between collaborative groups and the teacher, during which specific skills or goals are discussed. This feedback usually occurs spontaneously as the need arises.

The right kind of assessment at the right time can be a powerful aid to learning. When you design an assessment that flows naturally from instruction and student investigations, it isn't difficult to motivate students. Often they will view the assess-ment task not as an assessment at all, but simply as another learning activity.

Ms. Surong's Classroom

To demonstrate how the continuous learning cycle with student involvement might be put into effect in the classroom setting, let's envision a fifth-grade classroom that is about to embark on a unit.

Ms. Surong is teaching her students about genres in literature, using the following standard:

> Compare and contrast various genres of fiction (for example, mysteries, science fiction, historical fiction, adventures, fantasies, fables, myths) based upon their characteristics.

Ms. Surong has already analyzed the standard to determine what she needs to teach, how much in depth she needs to go, and what she expects students to know by the end of the unit. She will provide a lesson on each of the genres, so that her students will have enough background knowledge to identify its specific characteristics. Ms. Surong's first lesson is on science fiction.

Preassessing While Activating Prior Knowledge

She must first preassess the current knowledge level of her students. Some may start their learning at the *essential knowledge* level before proceeding to the standard's requirement, and some may begin their learning at a level well past the standard's requirement. Ms. Surong has decided that she will preassess her students as she activates their prior knowledge.

Ms. Surong begins the unit by holding up copies of *Star Wars, The Martian Chronicles,* and *The Land That Time Forgot;* she tells students that these are all examples of science fiction. Next, she ensures that students will feel some responsibility for the learning by pointing at the overall standard and the four goals they will learn by the end of the unit. She will refer to these goals often. Students are also given an Ongoing Student Self-Reflection Sheet that they will use throughout the learning process, so that they can reflect on their learning progress. She asks students to talk in cooperative groups about their current knowledge of science fiction stories. She then instructs them to create a list of characteristics that they believe to be true for science fiction. As students are talking and creating their lists, Ms. Surong walks around the room with a checklist, listening to student discussions and reading their science fiction attribute lists. She makes notes next to the names on her list indicating who has a high understanding, who has a fair understanding, and who has little or no understanding of science fiction.

Preteaching the Vocabulary of the Standard

In order to "preteach" some of the important concepts and terms in or related to the standard for science fiction, Ms. Surong meets with a small group of students who have little understanding of this genre. When they finish meeting, she provides vocabulary instruction for these terms for the whole class. Students who received the preteaching will benefit from this second learning opportunity. All students write these terms in their journal notebooks, add the definitions, and create a sketch or drawing to help them remember each term or concept.

Refer to *Words First: Learning the Language of the Standards,* volume two of this series, for detailed instructions on teaching the vocabulary of the standards.

Informal and Growth Assessments

As students learn about the characteristics of science fiction, Ms. Surong informally assesses them throughout the lesson. She gives them graphic organizers on which they make notes and sketches. In addition, she asks them many questions throughout the instruction and looks at their graphic organizers to assess their understanding. She then provides specific feedback to students regarding what they know well and in what areas they still need to work. At this point, these assessments are still informal and not intended to be used in student grades.

Following the instruction on science fiction characteristics, Ms. Surong asks students to write a two-paragraph essay about the important attributes of science fiction stories and to create a colorful poster to demonstrate some of these characteristics. This gives her additional opportunities to provide specific feedback regarding students' level of understanding. It will also show areas where she may need to provide further instruction. Ms. Surong will score the essay and poster with a rubric, which she gives students in advance; however, rather than serving as a grade, the rubric scores will most likely serve as student feedback and offer them opportunities to refine their work. If she feels confident that students understand the concepts, the rubric scores might be included as one of the pieces of the pie that lead to a grade at the completion of the lesson.

Final Student Product

When Ms. Surong feels her students are ready for the final assessment, she asks them to create oral presentations in groups of four. These presentations will demonstrate their understanding of science fiction characteristics through an actual story they have chosen. Although they are working in groups, each student in each group will be responsible for a particular component in the presentation, so that she can evaluate them on their individual proficiencies and deficiencies. Students will also reflect in their journals about their new learning.

Once Ms. Surong assesses student presentations and journal entries, she will know who needs further instruction and who is ready to move on to the next genre. She may also make note of specific characteristics of science fiction that were commonly misunderstood by a large number of students. This information helps her to focus her reteaching on areas of greatest need.

You can see from this story that assessment doesn't occur only at the end of the lesson. Ms. Surong began assessing student proficiency as she activated student prior knowledge, and she continued assessing student understanding throughout the lesson. One cannot talk about assessment without talking about the entire instructional cycle.

The Language of Assessment

Although it is often the same as the instructional language, to promote academic proficiency we must also help students become clear about the specific language that will be used when they are assessed. It's unreasonable to expect a person to reach high levels of learning when he or she has not learned the meanings of the words with which they will be taught and assessed. It's also imperative that teachers use the precise language that the content standard uses, because this will be the same language that students will see on the end-of-year standardized tests. Appropriate vocabulary instruction emphasizes *frequent words* (words that students see frequently), *content words* (terms that reflect the content standards, instructional language, or assignment language), and *challenging words* (words with more than one meaning, for example).

Although teaching the language of the content begins as an instructional strategy, it must also be discussed in the context of assessment; students need to learn the precise terms of the standards that are being taught. When all components in the instructional design—from stating the goals, to lesson instruction, to student practice, to final assessment—have spoken the language of the standard, then chances for achievement are increased through a deeper understanding and a successful final assessment.

Thinking About Your Thinking

Just as students must be versed in the language of their learning, educators must become fluent in the language of assessment. Becoming proficient with accurate assessment language enables teachers to design and institute effective measures of student—and teacher—success.

In helping you to focus on the language of assessment, we have chosen 17 *must know* words that will be helpful as you read each of the succeeding chapters. Use the reproducible terminology grid, Tool 1 in the Tools and Templates section, to help process these assessment terms. As the learner throughout this book, you will also benefit from reviewing these terms periodically.

Tools and Templates

The reproducible resources found in this section at the end of each chapter may also be found online at teachinginfocus.com.

Tool 1: Terminology Grid

As you read each term and definition, reflect on your own background knowledge and experiences to enhance your understanding of the term. First, share your thinking in the center box. Then, in the box on the right, create a symbol or other visual reminder that will help you to embed the term into your long-term memory.

WORD AND DEFINITION	YOUR THOUGHTS OR EXPERIENCES	YOUR VISUAL REMINDER
Content Standard: What students need to know and be able to do in various content areas such as mathematics, reading, writing, science, social studies, fine arts, comprehensive health, technology, foreign language, and workplace skills. Content standards may also be referred to as targets, benchmarks, performance objectives, outcomes, or goals.		
Formative Assessment: An ongoing process throughout the learning cycle to determine student understanding and teacher effectiveness. It should be a purposeful and natural process that coincides with instruction.		
Preassessment: Tools or activities used to measure student mastery of goals or standards prior to the instruction		
Informal Assessment: Tools or activities used to measure student progress and teacher effectiveness. These assessments are not used for grades, as students are not expected to have mastered goals at this point.		

(continued)

Focused Assessment © 2008 Solution Tree Press • solution-tree.com
Visit **teachinginfocus.com** to download this page.

Tool 1: Terminology Grid (continued)

WORD AND DEFINITION	YOUR THOUGHTS OR EXPERIENCES	YOUR VISUAL REMINDER
Growth Assessment: Tools or activities used to measure a benchmark mastery of portions of goals or standards. They may be translated into grades.		
Final Student Product: A cumulative final picture of students' understanding and mastery of a standard or goal		
Summative Assessment: A test or measurement of achievement usually given at the end of a unit, course, or program to judge student proficiency (for example, semester exams and standardized tests)		
Selected-Response Assessment: A test in which participants choose an option rather than create their own answer. Format examples include multiple choice, true/false, fill in the blank, and matching.		
Reliability: The extent to which an assessment is consistent. We need to strive for a reliable, consistent instrument to measure student achievement.		
Validity: The extent to which an assessment is accurate. This relates to content accuracy as well as test format accuracy.		
Performance Criteria: The guidelines, rules, characteristics, or attributes that are used to judge the quality of student performance		

(continued)

Tool 1: Terminology Grid (continued)

WORD AND DEFINITION	YOUR THOUGHTS OR EXPERIENCES	YOUR VISUAL REMINDER
Performance Assessment: A demonstration of student understanding through relevant or authentic tasks, processes, or products. The performance criteria (or rubric) may be used for scoring		
Rubric: A scoring tool that lists the performance criteria that will be used to judge student work and the degrees of quality for a piece of work		
Layered Learning: The depth of understanding that students are expected to achieve. The layered categories are essential knowledge, application, and complex thinking.		
Customized Assessment: Assessments created by the teacher that meet the needs of each unique learner		
Continuous Learning Cycle: A cycle of instruction and assessment in which all phases of teaching, learning, and measures of student success are in a dynamic and mutually enriching relationship		
Professional Learning Community*: A collaborative team whose members work interdependently to achieve common goals, with an emphasis on learning rather than teaching		

*From DuFour, DuFour, Eaker, and Karhanek, 2004.

Tool 2: Terminology Reflections

Take some time to determine what you currently know based on your experiences and the terminology section from chapter 1. Then make a list of what you would like to know more about.

WHAT I KNOW	WHAT I WANT TO KNOW
Share your understandings of formative assessment.	
To what degree does the concept of formative assessment correspond to your own thinking about assessment?	
Share your thoughts about customizing the assessment through the use of essential, application, and complex-thinking layers of learning.	

Tool 3: Ongoing Student Self-Reflection

Student Directions: Use this sheet multiple times in order to see improvements as well as uncover areas that need additional work.

Performance Task:			
Performance Criteria:			
Date:	In comparing my work to the criteria, these are my strengths:	In comparing my work to the criteria, these are my weaknesses:	Here are my next steps toward reaching the targets:

Tool 4: Comparing Formative and Summative Assessment

TYPE OF ASSESSMENT	FORMAT
Formative Assessment Ongoing, varied, a tool for learning and diagnosing	**Performance Assessments** Essay, journal, presentation, report, diorama, poster, and so on **Selected Response** Multiple choice, true/false, fill in the blank, matching
Summative Assessment A single test, usually given at the end of a lesson, unit, or semester, to measure achievement	**Selected Response (most likely format)** Multiple choice, true/false, fill in the blank, matching **Performance Assessments** Essay, journal, presentation, report, diorama, poster, and so on

2

Laying the Groundwork

Educational improvement must begin with a clear idea of what students are expected to learn. This premise underlies the standards-based efforts to improve American education.

—Robert L. Linn and Norman E. Gronlund

In this chapter . . .

- Thinking About Assessment
- Reviewing Prior Data
- Analyzing the Standard
- Teaching the Vocabulary of the Standard
- Thinking About Your Thinking
- Tools and Templates

Thinking About Assessment

As you consider moving to a focused assessment approach, ask yourself the following questions: Who will be involved in creating and implementing assessments? Will your grade-level team work collaboratively? How involved will students be?

Reviewing Prior Data

In the standards-driven system in which we are now teaching, each educator is responsible for an abundance of standards and goals. The task of deciding how much time to spend teaching and assessing each one can be daunting, to say the least.

This chapter will share ideas and strategies for helping you to begin the tasks of prioritizing your standards and determining where to focus more time and energy as you strive to meet the needs of all learners.

Whether you are a classroom teacher developing assessment on your own or part of a teacher team, the first step as the school year or semester begins is to analyze prior student data to determine where the student deficiencies are, so you know which areas to concentrate on. If you teach seventh-grade algebra, for example, you would study data from incoming students' sixth-grade assessments. This could include portfolio work, district benchmark assessments, or end-of-year standardized tests.

To activate your prior knowledge regarding the analysis of summative assessment results, study the test scores in Table 2-1. The table is set up for a third-grade teacher studying second-grade test scores. How would you use this information to create formative assessment and in-depth content coverage?

Table 2-1. Grade 2 Math Proficiency

GRADE 2 CLASSES	NUMBER SENSE & OPERATIONS	MATH STRUCTURE & LOGIC	DATA ANALYSIS & PROBABILITY	PATTERNS, ALGEBRA, & FUNCTION	GEOMETRY & MEASUREMENT
Ms. Thompson	75%	55%	60%	45%	72%
Mr. Wright	81%	65%	55%	49%	65%
Ms. Norton	78%	58%	58%	39%	67%
Ms. Krantz	69%	59%	56%	53%	74%
Mr. Olivas	79%	54%	50%	48%	81%

Without even getting out your calculator, you can see that the math categories in which the greatest percentage of students were successful were number sense and operations and geometry and measurement. Students had the lowest percentage of success in the categories of patterns, algebra, and function. This does not mean you would focus all your energies during the school year *only* on these high-need standards, but that these are areas into which you would delve more deeply and spend more time. In addition, you need to consider these other important and possibly mitigating factors:

- Has the school created focus goals for essential standards other than those that you have determined are a main focus?

- Based on district tests, state tests, and high-school exit tests, which areas of the academic content are weighted most heavily?

Begin your quest by looking at such norm- and criteria-referenced tests as the following:

- Local assessments—teacher-made tests and school-developed assessments. How well did students perform in the various academic areas represented on these tests? Which of the low-performing areas are heavily weighted on the district, state, and national assessments?

- District assessments—the TerraNova and Otis-Lennon School Ability tests, to name just two possibilities. How well did individuals and groups of students perform in the areas in which they were tested? On which specific test items or questions did a high percentage of students score poorly?

- State tests—for example, the Illinois Standards Achievement Test, California Achievement Test, Iowa Test of Basic Skills, and Stanford Achievement Test.

Reviewing James Armstrong's Data

Now let's assess your skill at analyzing this kind of data one more time. Suppose you are a ninth-grade language-arts teacher studying the eighth-grade end-of-year test scores. Table 2-2 on page 30 depicts one student's reading and writing strengths and weaknesses. If his test score results were typical of the new group of students that you are receiving, where might you want to focus your assessments and in-depth teaching?

Table 2-2. Standardized Student Test Scores for James Armstrong

GRADE 8	GRADE EQUIVALENT	SCALE SCORE	NATIONAL STANINE	NATIONAL PERCENTILE	RANGE
Reading Fluency	7.8	746	5	58	48–68
Reading Comprehension	11.1	781	7	84	74–89
Expository Writing	8.1	771	7	75	55–75
Expressive Writing	7.1	738	5	50	43–63

Grade Equivalence

Starting with James's grade-level equivalent score, there are several important factors to consider. If we take these numbers literally, and if this test was given at the end of the previous year, then all of James's scores with the exception of reading comprehension miss the grade-level mark. Even expository writing that shows a grade-level equivalency of eighth grade, first month, would be short by several months from being on track. However, there is more to reading grade-equivalency scores than meets the eye. These scores compare student performance on reading and writing only to the scores of those students who took the *same* test. In other words, these numbers were based only on those grade levels that were administered the eighth-grade test. So while impressive on the surface, the 11.1 that James received in reading comprehension does not necessarily mean that he is truly ready to read and comprehend 11th-grade text, because he was not compared to 11th-grade students. We know only that he excels in eighth-grade reading comprehension.

Scale Score

Scale scores can be used to study student performance changes over time. However, a student may have an increase in scale scores from one year to the next, while not necessarily performing at the same or a greater percentile level. Scale scores are quite technical and not very useful in analyzing classroom data.

National Stanine

National stanine is a slightly less precise yet easier-to-decipher score. A stanine is usually a nine-point scale created from a normal distribution of scores. The first stanine is the lowest scoring group, and the ninth stanine is the highest scoring group. So in interpreting James's stanine score, we could say that James's reading fluency is in the average range in terms of the norm group's performance.

National Percentile

Let's look at the national percentile score next. This number tells us the percent of students in the norm group that James outscored in a range from 0 to the 99th percentile. Put more simply, in reading fluency, James outscored 55% of the students who took the test. In the category of expository writing, James outscored 75% of the students who took the test.

Range

The range scores tell us that if James took this same test multiple times, he could be expected to score within the listed percentile ranges. For example, in the category of reading fluency, if James took the test again, he is predicted to score somewhere between the 48th and 68th percentiles. (Disregard the scale score column if it appears on norm-referenced tests, as it is not relevant for classroom-assessment score analysis.)

In looking at the whole picture of James's assessment scores, we see some trends that may help us to better teach and assess James as he moves into our ninth-grade classroom. He performed significantly higher in reading comprehension than in reading fluency. This tells us not to be fooled by slower or less than fluent oral reading. What he reads, he understands! We also know that James's expressive writing is a full grade level below that of his expository writing. This might indicate a writing and reading preference for factual, informational text over fiction and fantasy, and could give us some insight as we begin to make plans to differentiate for all learners. Since James has high comprehension skills but slightly below-level expressive writing skills, you might at some point create a collaborative group in which James could guide students with content information while another student strong in expressive writing could guide the group in using creative language and expression.

Ms. Maro's Seventh-Grade Classroom

Seventh-grade language-arts teacher Juanita Maro from Millworth Middle School decided to use data from two different assessments in order to determine her highest priorities for the creation of formative assessments.

First, she gathered class test scores from the sixth-grade, end-of-course district reading test. Table 2-3 shows rubric scores over points possible.

Table 2-3. Millworth Middle School End-of-Course Reading Test 2008 (Based on District Rubric Assessment)

TEACHER	LITERARY WRITING	EXPOSITORY WRITING	FUNCTIONAL WRITING	PERSUASIVE WRITING	RESEARCH WRITING
Scholtz	20/25	19/25	17/25	20/25	15/25
Wentworth	19/25	17/25	20/25	16/25	14/25
Ong	21/25	21/25	18/25	19/25	17/25
Jenkins	17/25	19/25	18/25	20/25	18/25
Washington	21/25	16/25	17/25	19/25	15/25
Hernandez	15/25	19/25	19/25	20/25	12/25
Lincoln	19/25	18/25	20/25	19/25	17/25
Desoto	18/25	21/25	19/25	20/25	16/25
Average of Each Genre	18.75	18.75	18.50	19.00	15.50

Next, Ms. Maro looked at portfolio assessment samples from the previous year to determine student writing abilities in the different writing traits. She found samples for many of the traits for which she is trying to determine the greatest need. Table 2-4 is a copy of the rubric that the sixth-grade teachers used to score a persuasive essay. Following the rubric, in Tables 2-5 and 2-6, respectively, on pages 34 and 35, are one student's self-assessment and the teacher's assessment of her own proficiency.

Table 2-4. Instructional Rubric for a Persuasive Essay*

GRADATIONS OF QUALITY			
CRITERIA	**4**	**3**	**2**	**1**
The claim	I make a claim and explain why it is controversial.	I make a claim but don't explain why it is controversial.	My claim is buried, confused, or unclear.	I don't say what my argument or claim is.
Reasons in support of the claim	I give clear and accurate reasons in support of my claim.	I give reasons in support of my claim, but I overlook important reasons.	I give one or two weak reasons that don't support my claim, or else I give irrelevant or confusing reasons.	I don't give reasons in support of my claim.
Reasons against the claim	I discuss the reasons against my claim and explain why it is valid anyway.	I discuss the reasons against my claim but neglect some or don't explain why the claim still stands.	I say that there are reasons against the claim, but I don't discuss them.	I don't acknowledge or discuss the reasons against my claim.
Organization	My writing has a compelling opening, an informative middle, and a satisfying conclusion.	My writing has a beginning, a middle, and an end.	My organization is rough but workable. I may sometimes get off topic.	My writing is aimless and disorganized.
Voice and tone	It sounds like I care about my argument. I tell how I think and feel about it.	My tone is okay, but my paper could have been written by anyone. I need to tell how I think and feel.	My writing is bland or pretentious. There is either no hint of a real person in it, or it sounds like I'm faking it.	My writing is too formal or informal. It sounds like I don't like the topic of the essay.
Word choice	The words that I use are striking but natural, varied, and vivid.	I make some fine and some routine word choices.	The words that I use are often dull or uninspired or sound like I'm trying too hard to impress.	I use the same words over and over. Some words may be confusing.
Sentence fluency	My sentences are clear, complete, and of varying lengths.	I use well-constructed sentences. My essay marches along but doesn't dance.	My sentences are often awkward, run-ons, or fragments.	Many run-on sentences and sentence fragments make my essay hard to read.
Conventions	I use correct grammar, punctuation, and spelling.	I have a few errors to fix, but I generally use correct conventions.	I have enough errors in my essay to distract a reader.	Numerous errors make my paper hard to read.

*Adapted from Goodrich, 2000.

Table 2-5. Persuasive Essay Rubric Scores for Linda Rubio

CRITERIA	STUDENT SELF-ASSESSMENT	TEACHER'S ASSESSMENT
The claim	4—I made my persuasion claim and told why it was controversial.	4—The claim that was made was clearly explained, and the reasons why it was controversial were clearly explained.
Reasons in support of the claim	4—I gave very clear reasons to support my statements.	3—Clear reasons were given to support the claim, but one of them was not accurate.
Reasons against the claim	3—I gave reasons against my claim but forgot one of them.	3—The reasons against the claim were clear but not sufficient.
Organization	4—I had a good opening, an informative middle, and a satisfying conclusion.	3—The writing had a clear beginning, middle, and end but lacked satisfying and pertinent information.
Voice and tone	4—I definitely cared about my argument. I told exactly how I feel about it.	4—The paper showed some passion regarding the topic and claim.
Word choice	3—I made some fine and some routine word choices.	3—The paper showed both interesting and routine word choices.
Sentence fluency	4—My sentences were clear, complete, and of varying lengths.	4—The sentences were clear, complete, and of varying lengths.
Conventions	4—I used correct grammar, punctuation, and spelling.	3—Some grammar and spelling errors were noted.

Both the district rubric scores as well as the individual assessments in which students and teachers ranked student proficiency showed that students overall were proficient with persuasive essay writing. After carefully reviewing the district language-arts assessment and the sixth-grade portfolio with writing samples in a variety of genres, Ms. Maro decided that she would need to designate more time for the writing of research papers this year, since students overall showed the lowest performance in that area. She justified her decision by creating the Focus on Standards form shown in Table 2-6, which she shared with the principal.

Table 2-6. Focus on Standards

WRITING GENRE	ACTION PLAN
Literary	Start in first quarter as planned.
Expository	Continue with third-quarter plan.
Functional	Integrate throughout all quarters, but highlight in fourth quarter.
Persuasive	Move to fourth quarter and spend only 2 weeks on this.
Research	Area of greatest need: 1) Move this to second quarter in order to spend more time on it. 2) Analyze the standards. 3) Create formative assessment plan. 4) Implement research unit. 5) Review data throughout unit, and adjust instruction and student activities as needed.

Once you determine areas of weakness that affect a large portion of students, or areas that are weighted heavily on district and state tests, you are ready to analyze the standards to determine those of greatest need. Again, this doesn't mean that you will ignore all other standards, but rather that some standards require in-depth coverage.

Analyzing the Standard

In *Focused Instruction,* volume one of the Teaching in Focus series, we discussed the need for teachers to analyze content standards by categorizing them into three layers of learning, based on the knowledge depth that they expect their students to achieve. These layers are the *essential knowledge, application,* and *complex-thinking layers.* Next, the teacher must determine which students are ready for the standard as it is written and which students need to begin at either a less or more challenging level.

Analyzing the standard will allow you to determine the following with precision:

• What you need to teach

- What students are expected to know by the end of the lesson and the extent to which they are expected to know it

- How you can differentiate both the learning and the assessment most effectively

In an ideal world, we would simply analyze the standard, determine the depth with which we need to teach a particular standard, and then teach it, assess it, and move on. But in the real world, we often have over 30 students in our classrooms, each with their own strengths and weaknesses and their own unique social, emotional, and academic needs. If you determine that a particular standard is asking students to reach a complex-thinking level—the highest achievement level—you'll no doubt find that many of your students will not be ready to go there. But by taking the time to analyze the standard, you will be able to bring all of your students to this level in stages. In other words, some students will need basic or *essential* instruction prior to the teaching of the higher level content or skills. Another group can now *apply* the content or skills but aren't quite ready for the higher level of complex or critical thinking skills. Still another group of high achievers may be ready immediately to learn, apply, and effectively employ *complex thinking.* Your assessments may similarly be customized. Perhaps you will create a rubric or a selected-response assessment for each of the three groups of students, according to their readiness. In this way, all your students can reach the expectations of the standard in progressive steps.

Looking at the Verbs

How do you analyze the standard? First, look closely at the verbs to determine the depth of learning required. Verbs suggesting passive actions, such as *know, understand,* or *identify,* indicate that the standard is calling for essential knowledge or understanding.

Standards that ask students to apply their knowledge will have more active verbs such as *write, read, determine, sequence,* or *decide.*

The third layer of learning expects students to use complex-thinking skills and uses verbs such as *analyze, synthesize, self-assess,* and *make judgments.* Complex thinking usually refers to processes that help to adjust and direct learning and consists of students' planning and monitoring their cognitive activities, as well as checking the outcomes of those activities and making judgments about them.

Noting the level of learning that students are expected to achieve helps teachers make decisions about their instructional and assessment practices and the ways they need to differentiate. Here, for example, are three levels of a standard dealing with historical timelines:

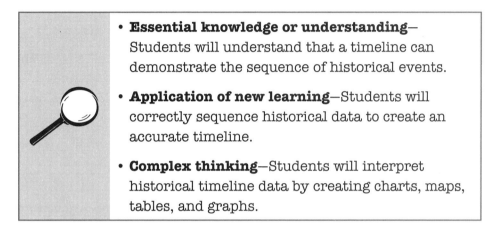

- **Essential knowledge or understanding—** Students will understand that a timeline can demonstrate the sequence of historical events.

- **Application of new learning**—Students will correctly sequence historical data to create an accurate timeline.

- **Complex thinking**—Students will interpret historical timeline data by creating charts, maps, tables, and graphs.

In the *essential knowledge* category, students are simply expected to understand what a timeline is and does. In the second example, students must *apply* their knowledge by correctly sequencing the events in a timeline. Then, at the *complex-thinking level,* students must be able to interpret a timeline in order to create a product.

Let's review the process of focused assessment up to this point:

1. You reviewed prior assessment data to determine the standards on which you want to focus.

2. You chose the standard of greatest concern as you began the process of creating formative assessments.

3. You analyzed that standard to determine the layer of learning being called for.

4. You customized your assessment in order to assess students at their layer of readiness, whether it's below or above the expectation of the standard, with the goal in mind that everyone in your class will eventually meet it.

Teaching the Vocabulary of the Standard

Now you must choose the terms that will be most crucial for students to know in order to be successful. Let's see how this works at a typical elementary school.

Shoshone Elementary School

Third-grade teachers at Shoshone Elementary are working together to create common assessments. After reviewing test scores from the previous year, they determined that the math standard *geometric properties* was the area of greatest need. Once they analyzed the standard and created three layers of learning, they then decided which terms and concepts students would need to be fluent in to be successful with the goals of the learning.

Words of the Standard

The group began by choosing words that came directly from the wording of the standard. This turned out to be most of them, as they wanted to make sure that their students were very clear about the learning expectations. The teachers wrote the exact standard on their classroom whiteboards and, as one of the first activities of the unit, engaged their students in analyzing it as a class and creating a simplified version of it that made sense to them. The teachers wrote this easier version underneath the original and left both of them on the whiteboard for the duration of the unit.

Standard: Concept 1—Geometric Properties

Analyze the attributes and properties of two- and three-dimensional shapes, and develop mathematical arguments about their relationships.

Easier Version:
Thoroughly examine two- and three-dimensional shapes and develop mathematical arguments about their relationships.

Frequent Words. The group then looked at both the standard and at the goals underneath it for the words that they suspected the students would be hearing frequently—words that would come up in oral instruction or written assignments.

Content Words. Under the content words column, the team wrote specific words found throughout the five goals under the standard. They also wrote words related to the content words that weren't directly written in the standard, as in the following example:

Standard: Concept 1—Geometric Properties

Goal 1: Build geometric figures with other common shapes (for example, tangrams, pattern blocks, and geoboards).

Goal 2: Name concrete objects and pictures of three-dimensional solids (cones, spheres, and cubes).

Goal 3: Describe relationships between two- and three-dimensional objects (squares/cubes, circles/spheres, triangles/cones).

Goal 4: Recognize similar shapes.

Goal 5: Identify a line of symmetry in a two-dimensional shape.

Challenging Words. Finally, the team looked for words that could be confusing, because they have more than one meaning. Remember, they were not concerned if they repeated words—if a word appeared in more than one column, it simply meant it would be emphasized and revisited often.

Creating a Bulletin Board. The group decided to create a bulletin board in each classroom that would depict the word list in Table 2-7 on page 40. They would start when they introduced the unit by putting up only the words of the standard. Then, as they began goal 1, they would add the goal 1 words to the bulletin board, and they would continue adding words with each new goal introduced. Although teaching the vocabulary with each new goal would take valuable time away from the lesson, the team had read enough of the research to realize that the language of the standard was a crucial component for student success.

Table 2-7. Adding Words for Each New Goal

WORDS OF THE STANDARD (WORDS TAKEN DIRECTLY FROM THE WORDING OF THE STANDARD)	FREQUENT WORDS (WORDS STUDENTS WILL SEE OR HEAR OFTEN)	CONTENT WORDS (WORDS THAT REFLECT THE CONTENT, INSTRUCTIONAL, OR ASSIGNMENT LANGUAGE)	CHALLENGING WORDS (WORDS WITH MORE THAN ONE MEANING)
Standard: Analyze, attributes, properties, two- and three-dimensional shapes, relationship, arguments	See specific goals below.	See specific goals below.	See specific goals below.
Goal 1: Geometric, common, tangrams, pattern blocks, geoboards	Sort, classify, identify, recognize, common shapes	Solids, flip, rotate	Common, sort, figures, relationship
Goal 2: Cones, spheres, cubes	Three-dimensional	Cones	Concrete
Goal 3: Squares, cubes, circles, spheres, triangles, cones	Two- and three-dimensional, relationships	Sides, lines, vertices, angles	Compare
Goal 4: Similar	Attributes, characteristics	Equal length, unequal length	Compare
Goal 5: Line of symmetry	Equal	Mirror image, halves	Relationship

Is It Worth It?

Teaching the language of the standard does take time away from the lesson, and at first it may seem like a monumental chore. But there are two benefits to keep in mind. First, studies show that there are significant achievement gains. Students learn the content more quickly and in greater depth because of the time that you took to ensure that they can speak the language in which they will be taught (Daneman, 1991; Kendall & Marzano, 1999).

Second, once students have mastered the procedures that you use to teach the vocabulary—and we suggest you choose several high-impact methods that benefit various learning styles—the time taken for this portion of your lessons will diminish greatly, and you'll have more time for content instruction. Whenever you feel frustrated about the amount of time that the vocabulary instruction takes, remember that 80–90% of what standardized tests assess is directly related to the language and concepts of the standard (Kendall & Marzano, 1999). In other words, if you did nothing more than teach the vocabulary of the standard, your students would be proficient with 80–90% of what the standardized test asked of them!

Thinking About Your Thinking

In this chapter we shared some important considerations:

- Who will be involved in creating and implementing formative assessments?
- How will you analyze prior data to determine greatest needs for formative assessment?
- Why is it critical that students know the language of the standard in order to be successful with assessment?

As a simple exercise, consider the content area that you teach. Based on assessment scores and your current knowledge of district goals, what would you guess to be the area of most need? What might come in second as being the next priority?

Tools and Templates

You can also find the reproducible tools and templates in this section online by going to teachinginfocus.com.

Tool 5: Focus on Standards

This exercise is used to prioritize those standards that, after an analysis of prior student data, need in-depth coverage and attention.

STRAND / SUBJECT / CONTENT	ACTION PLAN
	When will you teach? What actions will you take?
	When will you teach? What actions will you take?
	When will you teach? What actions will you take?
	When will you teach? What actions will you take?
	When will you teach? What actions will you take?

Tool 6: Choosing the Words of Focus

WORDS OF THE STANDARD (WORDS TAKEN DIRECTLY FROM THE WORDING OF THE STANDARD)	FREQUENT WORDS (WORDS STUDENTS WILL SEE OR HEAR OFTEN)	CONTENT WORDS (WORDS THAT REFLECT THE CONTENT, INSTRUCTIONAL, OR ASSIGNMENT LANGUAGE)	CHALLENGING WORDS (WORDS WITH MORE THAN ONE MEANING)
Standard:	See specific goals below.	See specific goals below.	See specific goals below.
Goal 1:			
Goal 2:			
Goal 3:			
Goal 4:			
Goal 5:			
Goal 6:			
Goal 7:			
Goal 8:			

Focused Assessment © 2008 Solution Tree Press • solution-tree.com
Visit **teachinginfocus.com** to download this page.

From Learning Targets to Assessments

Student learning research has repeatedly demonstrated the impact of assessment on student approaches to learning. . . . Ask them to understand the physics and chemistry of muscle contraction, but test them on the names of the muscles, and they will "learn" the names but not be able to explain how contraction happens.

—Peggy Nightingale and Mike O'Neil

In this chapter . . .

- Thinking About Assessment
- Performance vs. Selected-Response Assessments
- Performance Criteria
- From Performance Criteria to Rubric
- Using Essays to Test the Essential Knowledge Layer of Learning
- Using Selected Response to Test the Application and Complex-Thinking Layers
- Thinking About Your Thinking
- Tools and Templates

Thinking About Assessment

What do you want students to know or be able to do at the end of the lesson? In answering this question, you will need to consider your learning target, lesson goal, or curriculum standard. Do you know which layer of learning the standard or learning goal is asking for? Have you determined which students will need to start at the essential knowledge layer of learning before they will be ready to meet the standard expectation, and which vocabulary terms they will need to know to be successful? Have you thought about how you will customize the lessons? We want all students to reach the ultimate learning targets, but first we must be crystal clear about what our targets are, the path that each student will take to reach them, and how each student will demonstrate his or her learning.

Performance vs. Selected-Response Assessments

The two assessment formats we primarily discuss throughout this book are *performance assessments* and *selected-response assessments*. When the standard is calling for the essential knowledge layer of learning, usually a selected-response format is chosen. In this format, students demonstrate their understanding of what they know by filling in a blank, matching the concept to the definition, or choosing A, B, C, or D in a multiple-choice test. An example follows.

Learning Target: Identify key elements of a story including characters, setting, and plot.

Sample Selected-Response Assessment Item: Which is the most accurate description of the story's setting?

    A. Colonial America

    B. European Renaissance

    C. Modern-day America

    D. Modern-day Europe

Because essential knowledge usually involves the assessment of facts, concepts, or concrete knowledge, it can easily be assessed with a selected-response format. Some might argue that students engage in deeper learning when we ask them to share their knowledge in an essay rather than a selected-response assessment—and they are correct. We advocate the use of performance assessment formats when at all possible. Even essential knowledge can be very effectively assessed through journals, concept maps, and essays. The trick in using these formats, as we will see, is to make sure you assess *only* the essential knowledge. Of course there may be times, due to short class periods, lack of teacher planning time, and other time factors, when a selected-response format is the most effective way to assess.

When the standard is calling for the application or complex-thinking layer of learning (the student will *determine, interpret, judge, create* . . .), a performance format is almost always a more effective choice. An example standard and performance assessment item follow.

 Create a new setting that would change the outcome of the story.

Performance Assessment Item: In a short essay, create a new setting for this story that would have helped the characters to find their way home.

You can see that a target that asks students to create a setting change would be more difficult to assess with a selected-response assessment.

Later, we will also explore the two counterintuitive examples: using performance formats with essential knowledge standards and using selected-response formats with application or complex-thinking standards. But first, let's turn our attention to the essential building block of any assessment, regardless of format—the performance criteria.

Performance Criteria

Performance criteria are the guidelines, rules, characteristics, or attributes that are used to judge the quality of student performance. For example, if you were planning a unit in which the final student product was a research paper, you might create the categories of *research, content, mechanics,* and *organization of information,* as in Table 3-1 on page 48. You would then describe and define all of the expectations related to these attributes. These categories would result in the creation of your performance criteria.

Table 3-1. Performance Criteria Example: Research Paper

Research
Use and Citation of Multiple Research-Based Resources
Content
Clear Evidence of Relevance to the Topic With Insightful Ideas and Concepts
Mechanics
Striving to Be Error-Free in Spelling, Grammar, Sentence Structure, Punctuation
Organization of Information
Strong Evidence of Logic, Sequence, and Clear Topics and Subtopics

Next, you might ask yourself the following questions:

- Did I connect performance criteria to the standards?
- Did I choose a manageable number of performance criteria (3–5)?
- Did I create performance criteria that are measurable and teachable?
- Did I describe the performance criteria clearly?

From Performance Criteria to Rubric

The next obvious step after creating the performance criteria is to create the performance rubric. A rubric lists the performance criteria that will be used to judge student work and the degrees of quality. Since you have already created the performance criteria, you only need to fill in the performance tasks with the degrees of quality. Take a look at the rubric in Table 3-2 on page 49, which has precise performance criteria attributes with descriptions and the degrees of quality expected.

Table 3-2. Rubric With Performance Criteria

PERFORMANCE CRITERIA	EXEMPLARY 3	PROFICIENT 2	NOVICE 1	SCORES
Research—Effective use and citation of multiple research-based resources	Student has effectively used and cited multiple research-based resources.	Student has somewhat effectively used and cited multiple research-based resources.	Student resources lack effectiveness.	
Content Information—Clear evidence of relevance to the topic with insightful ideas and concepts	Content is relevant, pertinent to the topic, with in-depth and insightful ideas and concepts.	Content is mostly relevant and pertinent to the topic, demonstrating clear ideas and concepts.	Content is lacking in relevance to the topic and/or doesn't sufficiently demonstrate essential ideas and concepts.	
Mechanics—Effort to be error-free in spelling, grammar, sentence structure, punctuation	Spelling, grammar, sentence structure, and punctuation show few or no errors.	Spelling, grammar, sentence structure, and punctuation show a fair amount of errors.	Spelling, grammar, sentence structure, and punctuation show significant errors.	
Organization of Information—Strong evidence of logic, sequence, and clear topics and subtopics	Paper shows strong evidence of logic, sequence, and topic/subtopics.	Paper shows some evidence of logic, sequence, and topic/subtopics.	Paper shows little evidence of logic, sequence, and topic/subtopics.	

The Time Factor

Research demonstrates again and again that performance assessments with rubric scoring guides enhance learning and give clear expectations. The down side of using a rubric to assess students is the time factor. It is usually much faster to create and score a selected-response assessment than it is to create and score a performance assessment with a rubric. Here are two suggestions to remedy the time crunch:

1. When it's feasible, use rubric templates that are quick and easy to fill in with performance criteria and performance tasks.

2. Use a comprehensive essay rubric in which the knowledge of the topic area can be altered to fit multiple tasks. Specific content goals can easily be added or substituted to create a more focused rubric. The essay rubric in Table 3-3 is an example of a tool that can be easily modified.

Table 3-3. Essay Rubric

Knowledge of Topic Performance Criteria: Clear and in-depth understanding of topic and deeper critical issues demonstrated. Opinions and ideas stem from extensive subject knowledge and understanding.	
5 Essay clearly demonstrates both expertise regarding topic and understanding of deeper critical issues. Opinions and ideas are grounded in subject knowledge.	
4 Essay demonstrates both knowledge of topic and some understanding of deeper critical issues. Opinions and ideas are generally grounded in subject knowledge.	
3 Essay demonstrates knowledge of topic but little understanding of deeper critical issues. Opinions and ideas are vague or are not grounded in subject knowledge.	
2 Essay demonstrates little or no familiarity with topic, and understanding of deeper critical issues is not evident. Opinions and ideas are lacking or are not grounded in subject knowledge.	
1 Essay demonstrates little or no familiarity with topic, and there is no evidence of deeper understanding.	
Essay Development Performance Criteria: Strong evidence of strategic and insightful development and planning of ideas, facts, and arguments with logic and sequence.	
5 Essay demonstrates strategic and insightful development and planning of ideas, facts, and arguments in logical, sequential paragraphs.	
4 Essay demonstrates development and planning of ideas, facts, and arguments in mostly logical, sequential paragraphs.	
3 Essay demonstrates little planning of ideas, facts, and arguments, but paragraphs are somewhat sequential.	
2 Essay demonstrates little or no planning, and paragraphs show only a trace of being logical and sequential.	
1 Essay demonstrates little or no planning, and paragraphs do not show any traces of being logical and sequential.	

(continued)

Table 3-3. Essay Rubric (continued)

Language Performance Criteria: Essay has been edited, showing fluency, effective use of language and vocabulary, and sentence structure.	
5 Essay has been edited for use of language; there is a strong demonstration of fluency, vocabulary, and correct sentence structure.	
4 Essay has been edited for use of language; there is some evidence of fluency, vocabulary, and correct sentence structure.	
3 Essay has been edited for use of language; there are some flaws with fluency, vocabulary, and sentence structure.	
2 Essay has been edited to a minimal degree; there are multiple flaws with fluency, vocabulary, and sentence structure.	
1 Essay has *not* been edited; there are numerous flaws with fluency, vocabulary, and sentence structure.	
Mechanics Performance Criteria: Punctuation, wording, capitalization, and grammar are used effectively and flawlessly.	
5 Essay demonstrates exemplary use of punctuation, wording, capitalization, and grammar.	
4 Essay demonstrates effective use of punctuation, wording, capitalization, and grammar.	
3 Essay demonstrates use of punctuation, wording, capitalization, and grammar to a somewhat accurate degree.	
2 Essay demonstrates ineffective use of punctuation, wording, capitalization, and grammar.	
1 Essay demonstrates little or no regard for punctuation, wording, capitalization, and grammar.	

Under the first performance criteria, *Knowledge of Topic,* specific content goals could easily be added or substituted to create a more focused rubric. You can see that with such slight modifications, this particular rubric could be used routinely for essay assessments.

Using Essays to Test the Essential Knowledge Layer of Learning

As noted earlier, some argue that since an essay involves a process (in this case the writing process) it is not appropriate for testing essential knowledge, which only involves *knowing, identifying,* or *understanding*. But that's where being a professional with good common sense comes in handy. Let's say, for example, that you're teaching the following standard:

> Recognize that England and Spain wanted to rule other areas of the world.

This standard is written in the essential knowledge layer (*recognize*); nevertheless, you want students to demonstrate their knowledge through a more meaningful assessment than a multiple-choice or fill-in-the-blank test. You elect to have students write an essay, knowing that you must be careful to assess *only* the essential knowledge of your students. Of course, students who are ready for the application or complex-thinking layers of learning may be more challenged, with a slightly different question or rubric, than those who are in the essential knowledge layer.

This is where analyzing the standard is critical. You must ensure that what you are assessing is clearly what the standard is asking you to assess. It wouldn't be fair, in this case, to assess the essay format, paragraph form, sentence structure, or mechanics of the writing. You need to create your performance task, and hence your rubric, so that it reflects the standard that you taught. The rubric in Table 3-4, for example, would be appropriate to assess an essay for this standard.

Table 3-4. Rubric for a Standard

STANDARD	FULL RECOGNITION	PARTIAL RECOGNITION	LITTLE OR NO RECOGNITION
Through written expression, student shows recognition that England and Spain wanted to rule other areas of the world.	Student essay clearly shows a strong recognition that England and Spain wanted to rule other areas of the world.	Student essay is somewhat vague in demonstrating recognition that England and Spain wanted to rule other areas of the world.	Student essay shows little or no recognition that England and Spain wanted to rule other areas of the world.

Notice that the performance task reflects only what the standard is actually calling for. The student is not required to demonstrate written fluency or to know what other areas of the world England and Spain wanted to rule.

Now, what if in conjunction with teaching this standard about England and Spain, you were also teaching students how to appropriately edit an essay using language, vocabulary, and sentence structure effectively? If this second objective were being taught simultaneously with the history objective, or if students had already been taught this standard, then your rubric could reflect both expectations, as in Table 3-5.

Table 3-5. Rubric for Multiple Standards

STANDARDS	FULL RECOGNITION	PARTIAL RECOGNITION	LITTLE OR NO RECOGNITION
Through written expression, student shows recognition that England and Spain wanted to rule other areas of the world.	Student essay clearly shows a strong recognition that England and Spain wanted to rule other areas of the world.	Student essay is somewhat vague in demonstrating recognition that England and Spain wanted to rule other areas of the world.	Student essay shows little or no recognition that England and Spain wanted to rule other areas of the world.
Essay has been edited, showing effective use of language.	Essay has been edited and demonstrates effective and appropriate language that is relevant to the topic.	Essay has been edited and demonstrates somewhat effective and appropriate language that shows some relevance to the topic.	Essay has been edited and lacks effective or appropriate language with little relevance to the topic.
Essay has been edited, showing effective vocabulary usage.	Essay has been edited and demonstrates effective and appropriate vocabulary usage that is relevant to the topic.	Essay has been edited and demonstrates somewhat appropriate vocabulary usage with some relevance to the topic.	Essay has been edited and lacks effective or appropriate vocabulary usage with little relevance to the topic.
Essay has been edited, showing effective use of sentence structure.	Essay has been edited and demonstrates effective and insightful use of correct sentence structure.	Essay has been edited and demonstrates somewhat effective use of correct sentence structure.	Essay has been edited and lacks effective use of correct sentence structure.

Using Selected Response to Test the Application and Complex-Thinking Layers

Although it is usually more effective to use a performance-based assessment with these two layers, you can use a selected-response assessment with the application layer when it is worded carefully. The questions, in this case, would be less of the *who, what, when, where* variety and more of the *how* and *why* variety. *How* and *why* questions may also be utilized in addressing the complex layer of thinking. However, the addition of a performance-based section would create a much more valid assessment for this level. The example that follows provides a model for creating effective selected-response questions.

Mr. Henry's History Class

Mr. Henry's seventh-grade students have been studying the events leading to the American Revolution. Here is the content standard that Mr. Henry is currently teaching:

> Students will read and make inferences regarding the poem "Paul Revere's Ride."

The standard expectations are calling for the application layer of learning, which would most effectively be evaluated with a performance assessment. But Mr. Henry would like to attempt to create a selected-response assessment along with a short essay to meet the different needs of his learners. Some will not yet be ready to make inferences, so he will create assessment questions that will assess the essential knowledge layer of learning. He knows that once his diverse learners have mastered the essential knowledge layer of learning, he will have to reteach and bring them to the application layer, since that is what the standard is calling for. Other students will need a greater challenge, and for them he will create assessment items that assess the complex-thinking layer of learning. After reading the poem, determine for yourself whether or not Mr. Henry was successful in creating selected-response assessment items that would meet the diverse needs of his students, and then test your own knowledge of what constitutes effective selected responses. As you do so, consult the guidelines on page 55 of Rick Stiggins' book *Student-Involved Assessment for Learning* (2005).

Designing Selected-Response Assessments

This information is based on the model in *Student-Involved Assessment for Learning*, by Rick Stiggins (2005).

General Guidelines for All Formats

- Items clearly written and focused
- Stems created in question form
- Lowest possible reading level
- Irrelevant clues eliminated
- Items reviewed by colleague
- Scoring key double checked

Guidelines for Multiple-Choice Items

- Determine type of knowledge (essential, application, complex thinking) and formulate questions accordingly.
- Ensure that the question stem is truly aligned with the objective.
- Use age appropriate vocabulary that is consistent with language of the standard.
- Write comprehensive stems with short response options.
- Avoid unnecessary details.
- Avoid negatives in the stems.
- Use only one best answer in the response options.
- Use plausible distracters.
- Avoid the use of "None of the Above," or "All of the Above."
- Keep the length of response options similar.
- Do not use *would* or *should* in stems.
- Use unbiased cultural references.

Guidelines for True/False Items

- The statement is entirely true or false as presented.

Guidelines for Matching Exercises

- Clear directions are given.
- The list of items to be matched is brief.
- List consists of homogeneous entries.
- Response options are brief and parallel.
- Extra response options are offered.

Guidelines for Fill-In Items

- A direct question/statement is posed.
- One or two blanks are needed to respond (never more than two).
- Length of blank is not a clue.

(continued)

Designing Selected-Response Assessments (continued)

The first three stanzas of "Paul Revere's Ride" follow; the entire poem can be readily accessed on the Internet.

> Listen my children and you shall hear
> of the midnight ride of Paul Revere,
> on the eighteenth of April, in Seventy-five;
> Hardly a man is now alive
> Who remembers that famous day and year.
>
> He said to his friend, "If the British march
> By land or sea from the town to-night,
> Hang a lantern aloft in the belfry arch
> of the North Church tower as a signal light,—
> One if by land, and two if by sea;
> And I on the opposite shore will be,
> Ready to ride and spread the alarm
> through every Middlesex village and farm,
> For the country folk to be up and to arm."
>
> Then he said "Good-night!" and with muffled oar
> Silently rowed to the Charlestown shore,
> Just as the moon rose over the bay,
> Where swinging wide at her moorings lay
> The Somerset, British man-of-war;
> A phantom ship, with each mast and spar
> Across the moon like a prison bar,
> And a huge black hulk, that was magnified
> By its own reflection in the tide.

(continued)

Designing Selected-Response Assessments (continued)

Layered Selected-Response Items for "Paul Revere's Ride"

Essential Knowledge Layer

1. What signal did Paul Revere ask his friend to use to let him know that the British were coming by land or sea?
   A. Blowing a horn
   B. A lantern in the belfry tower
   C. A shout and a whistle
   D. Firing a shotgun into the air

2. Into what town did Paul Revere ride at midnight?
   A. Belfry
   B. Lexington
   C. Concord
   D. Medford

3. What was the midnight message of Paul Revere?
   A. The British were coming.
   B. He was going to Lexington.
   C. It was time for the colonists to wake up.
   D. He was coming to town on his horse.

Application Layer

1. Why was Paul Revere waiting on the opposite shore of the North Church tower?
   A. He was hiding because the British were coming.
   B. He wanted to be ready to spread the warning to the farms and villages.
   C. He didn't have a boat to get to the North Church tower.
   D. He wanted to join the British when they arrived.

2. What did a second lamp in the belfry tower indicate?
   A. The British were on foot and near the village.
   B. Paul Revere needed to hurry home.
   C. The British were marching to Lexington.
   D. The British were arriving by sea.

3. What line from the poem lets us know that dark crows were floating in the ocean?
   A. "the line of black that bends and floats"
   B. "and only pausing to fire and load"
   C. "the Mystic meeting the ocean tides"
   D. "under the alders that skirt its edge"   *(continued)*

Designing Selected-Response Assessments (continued)

Complex-Thinking Layer

1. Read and analyze the eighth stanza of the poem. From which line would you draw the inference that the whole country was in jeopardy of being taken over by England's rule?
   A. "Struck out by a steed flying fearless and fleet"
   B. "Kindled the land into flame with its heat"
   C. "The fate of a nation was riding that night."
   D. "Broad and deep, / is the Mystic, meeting the ocean tides"

2. Analyze the following: "And the meeting house windows black and bare, / Gaze at him with a spectral stare, / as if they already stood aghast / at the bloody work they would look upon." What inferences can you make?
   A. Paul Revere is envisioning the battles that would take place when the British arrive.
   B. There was blood on the meeting-house windows.
   C. Paul Revere saw someone covered in blood standing inside the meeting house.
   D. Paul Revere noticed that the meeting house was empty.

3. What is the significance of the author's description of the "bleating of the flock, the twitter of the birds, and the morning breeze?" Which of the following is he showing us?
   A. That Concord was a lovely farm town and that people who were living there were very fortunate
   B. The contrast between the current peaceful tranquility of their lives as compared to the bloody battle that is about to take place
   C. That it must have been spring since there were birds twittering with a gentle morning breeze
   D. There is no real significance to this information.

Mr. Henry has consciously created assessment items to meet the needs of students in all three layers of learning. He may have English-language learners or special education students in his classroom that need to begin their understanding of the poem through the essential assessment of knowledge. He may also have gifted or high-achieving students who are ready for the challenging, complex-thinking questions that he created. Since the actual standard calls for the application level of learning, Mr. Henry's goal must be to eventually bring all students *at least* to that level of learning.

Designing Selected-Response Assessments (continued)

Examples and Nonexamples of Effective Selected-Response Assessments

 Now test your understanding of what constitutes effective selected-response assessments. Using the guidelines below, determine which of the two choices given is the example and which is the nonexample.

Multiple Choice

1. What did a second lamp in the belfry tower indicate?
   A. It indicated that the British were on foot and near the village.
   B. It indicated that Paul Revere needed to hurry home.
   C. It indicated that the British were marching to Lexington.
   D. None of the above

2. What did a second lamp in the belfry tower indicate?
   A. The British were on foot and near the village.
   B. Paul Revere needed to hurry home.
   C. The British were marching to Lexington.
   D. The British were arriving by sea.

True/False

1. When Paul Revere rode to Lexington, he knew there would soon be a bloody battle there.

2. When Paul Revere road to Lexington, a battle between the British and the colonists had already occurred.

Matching

| 1. Crossed the bridge to Medford | Twelve by the village clock |
| 2. Rode into Lexington and saw the meeting-house windows, black and bare | One by the village clock |

Fill in the Blank

1. Revere told his friend to hang a signal light in the North Church tower, saying, "One if by _____, and two if by _____."

2. "Hang a lantern aloft in the _____ of the _____ as a signal light, One if _____, and two if _____; And I on the opposite shore will be."

Discussion

In the multiple-choice questions, the second set is the effective example. In the non-example, the language is redundant ("It indicated . . .") and creates longer foibles than are necessary. In addition, the answers "None of the above" or "All of the above" should be used very sparingly.

True/false statements must be precise—a true answer must be entirely true. Here, the second choice is the example because it demonstrates a completely false answer. The battle most definitely had not occurred by the time Paul Revere rode into Lexington. Therefore, the foible is effectively written. The first choice, which is presumably a true answer, is not entirely true, as it is the author's opinion or imagination that Paul Revere envisioned "the bloody work they would look upon."

In the matching exercise, the first choice is the effective example. Response options and matching items should be as brief as possible; the nonexample is too wordy to be effective.

Lastly, the first choice is the effective example for the fill-in-the-blank exercise. Too many blanks cause confusion.

Mr. Henry could easily include a short essay that could be scored quickly with a rubric. The rubric should be given to students prior to the lesson so that they will be clear about what they are expected to learn and do after reading the poem. It might look something like the one in Table 3-6.

Table 3-6. Making Inferences

PERFORMANCE CRITERIA	EXEMPLARY	PROFICIENT	NOVICE	SCORE
Students will read and make inferences regarding the poem "Paul Revere's Ride." They will write a three-paragraph essay, with each paragraph demonstrating an inference related to a phrase in the poem.				
Inferences—Direct and insightful inferences are made for at least three phrases from the poem.	Student has included three or more phrases from the poem and provided direct and insightful inferences for each.	Student has included three or less phrases from the poem, showing some or little insight in the inferences for each.	Student has included less than three phrases from the poem, and little or no direct inferences are made.	
Content Information—Each paragraph focuses on one topic that clearly demonstrates a content understanding.	Student has created paragraphs that focus on one topic each and clearly demonstrate a content understanding.	Student has created paragraphs that focus on one topic each and demonstrate a limited degree of content understanding.	Student paragraphs do not demonstrate a specific focus on any one topic, and a content understanding is lacking.	
Mechanics—The essay is error free in spelling, grammar, sentence structure, and punctuation.	Spelling, grammar, sentence structure, and punctuation show few or no errors.	Spelling, grammar, sentence structure, and punctuation show a fair amount of errors.	Spelling, grammar, sentence structure, and punctuation show significant errors.	

Thinking About Your Thinking

A performance assessment such as an essay, project, product, journal reflection, science experiment, presentation, or artifact allows students to demonstrate their learning in relevant and meaningful ways. However, not all assessments can or should be this involved. Think about instances that would be most appropriate for performance assessments and instances when it might be more effective to use a selected-response assessment.

Tools and Templates

The resources in this section can also be found online at teachinginfocus.com.

Tool 7: Creating Performance Criteria

CREATING PERFORMANCE CRITERIA
Decide upon the standards that you will be assessing and the assessment format that you will be using. Then, create three to five performance criteria for the assessment (for example, *content, mechanics,* and *organization*). Next, ask yourself the following questions to determine the effectiveness of your performance criteria. Did I connect performance criteria to the standards? Did I choose a manageable number of performance criteria (3–5)? Did I create performance criteria that are measurable and teachable?
Performance Criterion 1:
Performance Criterion 2:
Performance Criterion 3:
Performance Criterion 4:
Performance Criterion 5:

Tool 8: From Performance Criteria to Rubric

List your performance criteria down the left side of the rubric. After reviewing and analyzing the standard expectations, write the degrees of quality under Exemplary, Proficient, and Novice.

PERFORMANCE CRITERIA	EXEMPLARY 3	PROFICIENT 2	NOVICE 1	SCORES

Tool 9: When Is an Essay an Appropriate Assessment?

With slight modifications, essay formats can be appropriate for each of the three layers of learning. Using the standard and essay questions written below, find the layer of learning that is most appropriate for the expectations of the essay.

Standard	Describe the basic structure of a cell, including: · Cell wall · Cell membrane · Nucleus
Essay questions to meet the needs of each learner	1. In two paragraphs, describe the function of each of the three cell components and make an argument for the most important cell component. 2. In two paragraphs, define each of the three cell components. 3. In two paragraphs, describe the basic structure of a cell.

In each box below, write the essay questions from above that would best meet the needs of the three layers of learning.

LAYERS OF LEARNING AND ASSESSMENT	ESSAY QUESTIONS
Essential Knowledge (Standards will use verbs such as *know, understand, identify.*)	
Application (Standards will include verbs such as *write, read, determine, sequence,* or *decide.*)	
Complex Thinking (Standards will include verbs such as *analyze, synthesize,* or *make judgments.*)	

Choosing From a Variety of Formats

Standards can be raised only by changes that are put into direct effect by teachers and pupils in classrooms. There is a body of firm evidence that formative assessment is an essential component of classroom work and that its development can raise standards of achievement. We know of no other way of raising standards for which such a strong prima facie case can be made.

—Paul Black and Dylan Wiliam

In this chapter . . .

- Thinking About Assessment

- Which Designs Are Most Appropriate?

- Summative Assessment

- Thinking About Your Thinking

- Tools and Templates

Thinking About Assessment

Ponder these questions: What do you believe are the most powerful factors that influence student success, and what role does formative assessment play? Which kinds of assessments involve active engagement from the learner, and which do you feel cause deeper learning? Which formats allow you to customize expectations for diverse learners?

Which Designs Are Most Appropriate?

The concept of focused assessment provides consistent checks and evaluations of what students know and how effectively we are teaching them, so that we have a focused idea of the readiness levels of the students in our classroom. To acquire that sharply focused picture, we need to use a variety of means. That is why assessments do not have one particular format. This section presents a variety of formative assessments and discusses how to make good decisions about the most effective ones to use, based on student needs and content standards.

Teacher Observation With Checklist

A teacher checklist is a graphic chart that contains content standards, goals, skills, or student behaviors that you want to monitor for a specific purpose—such as determining student improvement or lack of it.

When should I use it? You can use a teacher checklist to do the following:

- Monitor a certain skill or goal on a long-term basis.

- Quickly determine student understanding of a newly introduced concept or skill.

- Gain insights during practice times as students work in cooperative groups, individually, or through whole-class discussions.

- Adjust instruction or plan to reteach based on observations and checklist results.

- Scaffold lessons into essential, application, and complex-thinking layers.

Checklist #1

In this example, four different standards or goals are addressed in a first-grade classroom under the umbrella of "math concepts." This teacher uses the checklist throughout the semester as she watches students use manipulatives, work in groups, or work individually on a task. She writes down the dates of each of her observations (Table 4-1):

Table 4-1. Math Concepts

STUDENT NAMES	Identify whole numbers through 100 in or out of order.	Write whole numbers through 100 in or out of order.	Construct equivalent forms of whole numbers, using manipulatives or symbols, through 99.	Construct models to represent place value concepts for the ones and tens places.
Linda	10/12: Can only ID when in sequence 11/10: Proficient	10/12: Can write up to 30 11/10: Can write up to 60	11/05: Proficient with base blocks of 10s and 5s 11/14: Proficient	1/20: Proficient
Frankie	10/12: Proficient	10/12: Knows how, but eye-hand coordination is immature	11/05: Proficient	1/20: Proficient

Checklist #2

This example is closer to a rubric but much less complex. The teacher asks students to write a narrative based on imagined or real events, observations, or memories that include character, setting, plot, and sensory details, as shown in Table 4-2:

Table 4-2. Elements of a Narrative

	Yes	No
Character—Effectively developed		
Setting—Clearly described		
Plot—Engaging and based on imagined or real events, observations, or memories		
Sensory Details		
Clear Language		
Logical Sequence of Events		

Checklist #3

The teacher lists content standards or goals in the second column, as shown in Table 4-3. In the third, she lists the process by which students will meet the expectations of the standard. The teacher assesses students while they are in the process of the learning.

Table 4-3. Content and Process Expectations

STUDENT	CONTENT EXPECTATIONS	PROCESS EXPECTATIONS	YES/NO WITH DATES
Philippe	Classify animals by identifiable group characteristics: • Vertebrates— mammals, birds, fish, reptiles, amphibians • Invertebrates— insects, arachnids	Communicates observations, classifications, and thoughts through group discussion	Yes 10/7/08
	Compare the following observable features of living things: • Movement—legs, wings • Protection—skin, feathers, tree bark • Respiration—lungs, gills • Support—plant stems, tree trunks	Communicates observations, comparisons, and thoughts through whole-class discussion and journal entry	No—journal entry doesn't show clear comparisons. 10/15/08

Graphic Organizers and Representations

A graphic organizer is a visual planning tool that structures information. The information in a graphic organizer can be written or depicted through symbols or sketches. We know that many students of poverty and culturally diverse students tend to perform at higher levels when they can engage in visual and kinesthetic tasks. Students also benefit from the use of graphic organizers and representations by becoming actively involved in the learning.

When should I use them? Graphic organizers are especially appropriate when planning instruction for essential, application, and complex-thinking layers of learning, as they make it fairly easy to differentiate the learning There are three ways to use them in this way:

1. All students receive the same graphic organizer, but some students have theirs partially filled in for them.

2. All students receive the same graphic organizer, but some students are not required to use all sections of it.

3. A slightly different graphic organizer is created for each of the three layers of learning.

Graphic organizers can be used at different stages of learning. Let's look at the following types of graphic organizers:

- Advance

- Content

- SQ3R

- Semantic feature analysis

Organizer #1: Advance

Advance organizers are used before direct instruction as follows:

- To bridge the gap between what students already know and what they need to know

- To show relationships between terms and definitions

- To plan a project, research paper, or essay

- To let students know what they will be learning

- To present learning at various levels of abstraction to accommodate all learners

- To bridge the gap between what the learner already knows and what he or she needs to know

- To improve levels of understanding and recall

A specific model provided by Joyce, Weil, & Calhoun (2003), shares a three-phase plan for advance organizer use. In phase one, you clarify the aim of the lesson, present the advance organizer to your students, and prompt awareness of relevant knowledge. In phase two, you present the learning task or learning material and make explicit its organization and logical order. And in phase three, you use *integrative-reconciliation learning* and *active-reception learning*. Integrative reconciliation is meaningful learning in which the learner discerns relations between concepts, and active reception has to do with thinking purposefully during an activity and constructing one's own mental image (for example, you can ask learners to make summaries, point out differences, and relate to new examples with the organizer).

You might also give students vocabulary terms in an advance-organizer format prior to teaching your lesson so that they can "speak the language of the standard." Or, you might provide them with a prior knowledge organizer like the one in Table 4-4 on page 71, which allows them to make predictions prior to the learning using their own background knowledge and experience.

Table 4-4. Prior Knowledge Organizer

Instruction: Respond to each "cause" statement twice. First, make predictions about the effect prior to the lesson, and then share new knowledge after the lesson.		
PREDICTIONS BEFORE LESSON	CAUSE	EFFECT
	1954: Vietnamese forces occupy the French command post at Dien Bien Phu, and the French commander orders his troops to cease fire.	
	1961: President John F. Kennedy orders more help for the South Vietnamese government in its war against the Viet Cong guerrillas.	
	1962: In Operation Chopper, helicopters flown by U.S. Army pilots ferry 1,000 South Vietnamese soldiers to sweep an NLF stronghold near Saigon.	
	1964: The captain of the USS Maddox reports that his vessel has been fired on and that an attack is imminent.	

Organizer #2: Content

Ask students to use the organizer during the learning:

- To show relationships between ideas or facts
- To record ongoing learning in a visual way

The content organizer shown in Figure 4-1 is most effective during a content lesson, whether you are using direct instruction, a video clip, or a textbook. Ask students to fill in the topic, concept, or theme (for example, main events in the Vietnam war). Students can later use this organizer to create an essay that will serve as a final assessment for the lesson or unit.

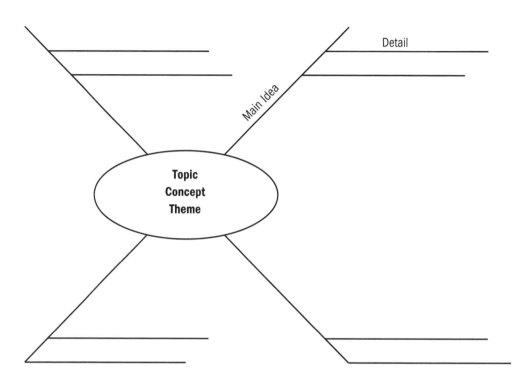

Figure 4-1. Content Organizer

After the learning, graphic organizers can be used to present or reflect on newly learned information and to determine what your students have learned and what more they still need to know.

Organizer #3: SQ3R

SQ3R stands for *Survey, Question, Read, Recite,* and *Review.* This graphic organizer, shown in Table 4-5, spans the entire lesson—beginning, middle, and end—and is extremely effective during the reading of nonfiction text. Use the Read, Recite and Review sections as an informal assessment.

Table 4-5. SQ3R

| Name _____ |
| Topic or Story Title: |

SURVEY	QUESTION	READ	RECITE
Record important titles and subtitles from chapter sections. _____	Write who, what, when, where, and why questions for the main topics and subtopics. _____	After reading, write answers to the five questions that were written. _____	Record additional interesting facts related to the five questions to complement the information that was discovered during the reading. _____

Review: Compose a one-paragraph summary for each of the questions that were answered. Use this as a study guide.

Organizer #4: Semantic Feature Analysis

Directions: To review a group of concepts, students fill in the boxes below with a "+" if the concept is associated with the attribute and a "–" if the concept is not associated with it.

CONCEPT: MAMMALS	ATTRIBUTES			
	Has live offspring	Has 4 legs	Has fur	Could live in your house
Dog	+	+	+	+
Grizzly Bear	+	+	+	–
Lizard	–	+	–	+ –
Fish	–	–	–	+ –
Horse	+	+	+	–

Essay Writing to Show Deeper Understanding

An essay generally combines information with informed opinions and consists of sentences and paragraphs that answer open-ended questions or problems. They are excellent for showing an understanding of concepts, principles, and ideas, and thus especially effective for the application and complex-thinking layers of learning. Essays can be as short as one paragraph or as long as several pages. Essay questions can measure a variety of skill objectives:

- Identifying cause and effect (application layer)

- Summarizing the main ideas and supporting details (essential knowledge and application layers)

- Creating a defense for a particular opinion (complex thinking)

- Analyzing (for example, character motivations, plot, causes for an event) (complex thinking)

- Comparing and contrasting (application)

- Making inferences (application and complex thinking)

- Reflecting on new understandings (application and complex thinking)

When should I use it? The beauty of using an essay for assessment is that it flows naturally from the instruction. For instance, if students complete a graphic representation during or after instruction, the next logical step is to ask them to use that representation to write an essay. Or, during the practice phase of instruction a teacher might assign an essay that students would then refine, edit, revise, and review prior to the final-draft essay—which would then serve as the final student assessment.

Here are specific guidelines for creating an effective essay assessment:

- Create questions that present a clear task directly related to the content standard or goal. Avoid *who, what, when,* and *where* questions, which don't lead to open-ended responses. Instead, ask students to *discuss, describe, explain, interpret, compare, contrast, make inferences, analyze, make judgments,* or *evaluate.*

- Provide three layers of essay questions in order to differentiate the assessment task. Engage all students in the same lesson content but differentiate the assessment, as in the following examples:

    1. Essential knowledge layer—After reading *The Abolitionist Movement*, explain what the abolitionist movement was about.

    2. Application layer—After reading *The Abolitionist Movement*, compare and contrast the accomplishments of two abolitionists in the 1800s Civil War era.

    3. Complex-thinking layer—After reading *The Abolitionist Movement*, make arguments for the abolitionist who you feel made the most difference in the antislavery movement. Then make inferences about what motivated this person.

- Provide students with an IDDC chart (Introduction, Detail Idea 1, Detail Idea 2, and Conclusion).

Refer to the chart in Figure 4-2 on page 76. An IDDC chart can help students organize their writing. You can differentiate this chart by creating some charts with only an IDC, while using an IDDC chart for more advanced students.

Teacher Questions

Questioning strategies involve knowing which students to call on, what types of questions to ask them (for example, essential knowledge, application, or complex thinking), and ways to respond or provide feedback to student answers.

When should I use them? Here are tips to follow when using questioning strategies:

- Think about the various questions you will ask as you analyze the standard and prepare your lesson plan. Determine a variety of questions for the different layers of learning.

- Ask questions clearly and specifically. Instead of "How did you like this story?" ask, "What did you like and what did you dislike about the story? Why?" Encourage students to expand on their answers and give reasons for their thinking.

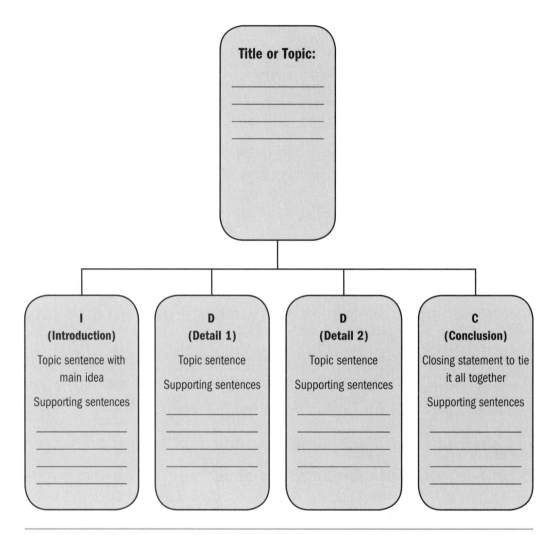

Figure 4-2. IDDC Chart

- Ensure that students understand the *language of the question.* Students cannot respond well to a question that contains unfamiliar terms.

- Ask questions from the various levels of Bloom's taxonomy of educational objectives. For a given standard that is being taught, ask students in the essential knowledge layer to *explain* or define it. Ask students in the application layer to *choose, decide,* or *determine.* Ask students in the complex-thinking layer to *make judgments about, synthesize,* or *evaluate.*

- Use questions to help students find relevance and make connections: "Now that we've learned about decimals, how can we compare them to fractions?"

- Use *open* questions to assess student current understanding. "Which part of the lesson was easy? Which part was difficult? Why?"

- Use a "wait time" of approximately 10–15 seconds after asking the question. Students need time to think and organize an answer before responding. You can also ask students to write down their response to a question. Next, call on several students to read their answers. This increases their level of concern and gets all students involved in the learning.

- Rephrase the question when it appears that a student does not understand.

The Three-Minute Talk

A 3-minute talk is a student's opportunity to reflect upon new learning, plan a presentation, and share new knowledge with others. When it is combined with the use of diagrams, artifacts, posters, computer-generated graphs or charts, or any other visual representations, it is a very powerful demonstration of learning.

Following are some characteristics of the 3-minute talk:

- It can be either impromptu or planned.

- It can be performed individually, with partners, or in small groups.

- The teacher provides specific criteria or questions to answer.

- The teacher provides a frame or organizer to help students to prepare for the "talk."

- Students create a visual to share during their talk.

Research shows that the oral explanation along with a visual representation taps into the following connections:

- Students are engaged in developing their own responses rather than selecting from predetermined options.

- Essential, application, and complex-thinking layers of learners can effectively use this assessment through simple differentiation techniques.

- A final product gives students a sense of real world or authentic learning.

- Classroom instruction or students' own investigation can be synthesized into an oral explanation.

- Clear criteria are made known to students throughout the process (by a rubric).

- Students learn to evaluate their own work.

- Student reflections on the learning transfer to new applications.

When should I use it? The use of a 3-minute talk when combined with visual representations that the student has created is a highly effective assessment practice for essential, application and complex-thinking layers of learners. However, we need to keep in mind the personality styles and intelligence strengths of our diverse learners. If one of your goals involves increasing student oral fluency, you will want to use this assessment format for all of your learners. However, for students who are intrapersonal and uncomfortable presenting information to the whole class, this format could be very stressful. A more comfortable modification for those learners would entail a small-group oral explanation.

Figure 4-3 shows a simple organizer that may be used multiple times in a variety of content areas.

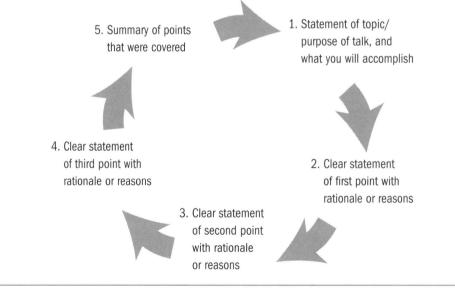

Figure 4-3. Three-Minute Talk Organizer

Kinesthetic Projects

A kinesthetic project is an assessment strategy that helps students combine academic content standards with relevant projects. With this approach, students move, create, and manipulate information as it is taken in. The teacher guides students to solve a problem or demonstrate their learning through a project on a display board, which may represent the culmination of various tasks or a big finale that is an entirely new creation, drawing on students' new learning. According to Robert Sylwester (1995), in *A Celebration of Neurons,* knowledge is retained longer if children connect not only orally but emotionally and physically to the material.

Research suggests that kinesthetic and authentic projects have several key characteristics (Donovan, Bransford, & Pellegrino, 1999):

- Learning is centered on authentic tasks that are of interest to the learners.

- Students are engaged in exploration and inquiry.

- Learning is usually interdisciplinary.

- Learning is closely connected to the world beyond the walls of the classroom.

- Students become engaged in complex tasks and higher-order thinking skills, such as analyzing, synthesizing, designing, manipulating, and evaluating information.

- Students produce a product that can be shared with an audience outside the classroom.

- Learning is student-driven, with teachers, parents, and outside experts all assisting/coaching in the learning process.

- Learners employ scaffolding techniques.

When should I use them? Kinesthetic projects should be used for the following goals:

- To foster and enhance the *personal interests* of the students that are tied to the curriculum—For example, if the content standard is related to reading fluency and comprehension, students could each explore reading materials of their own choice with a culminating kinesthetic project that demonstrates their learning.

- To enrich student understanding of the content standard to a much higher degree (complex thinking)

- To explore issues that tie into the curriculum (for example, space travel, historical conflicts, higher-level math concepts, and so on)

- To tie together all of the tasks that students have worked on during a particular unit

Kinesthetic projects generate student engagement in the learning, they are motivating and high interest, and unlike selected-response assessments, they generate additional learning and deeper meaning. An appropriate sequence for a kinesthetic project includes these steps:

1. Start by determining *what the standards are asking you to teach.* Analyze the standards to determine exactly what you need to teach, how much in depth you need to go, and what students are expected to know by the end of the lesson or unit, and then group them into the three layers—essential knowledge, application, and complex thinking.

2. Develop your performance criteria. For example, if you were planning a unit in which the final product would be a kinesthetic project, you might create performance criteria for the attributes of *research, content, mechanics,* and *organization of information.* Then describe and define all of the expectations related to the attributes. You will also want to differentiate the performance criteria based on the layers of learning. Ask students who are not ready to meet the expectations of a standard written at the application or complex-thinking layer to meet the performance criteria for the essential-knowledge layer. Once they have met that expectation, they can work toward meeting the actual standard expectation.

3. Create a rubric. The rubric lists the performance criteria that will be used to judge student work and the *degrees of quality* for a piece of work.

4. Determine the nuts and bolts of the project. This includes not only the materials and length of time needed, but also the process. Will students work alone or in groups? Will they be free to create the project according to their personal interests, or will all students follow the same plan?

5. Have students submit a project plan that both you and they can live with. This may entail a timeline, the materials needed, and a sketch that shows student goals for the outcome.

6. Decide on the audience with whom students may share their projects. Audiences may involve parents, teachers, other classes, or other classmates from your room.

7. Decide whether or not you will also include a selected-response assessment in addition to the project.

Students and teachers together can create project ideas based on learning styles, standard expectations, and differentiated layers of learning, like those shown in Table 4-6.

Table 4-6. Student-Choice Projects

Learning Target: Discuss human features (for example, cities, parks, railroads, hospitals, shops, schools) in the world.

	AUDITORY PROJECT	VISUAL PROJECT	KINESTHETIC PROJECT
Essential knowledge layer of learning	Helga—Two-minute oral presentation using classroom maps for examples Jose—Teacher-student conference so Jose can demonstrate human features in the world	Fara—Drawing that shows cities, parks, railroads, and so on, with labels	Cynthia—Shoebox diorama that includes cities, parks, railroads, and so on, with labels
Application layer of learning	Barbara—Three-minute oral presentation using overhead transparencies	Thomas—Drawing that shows cities, parks, railroads, and so on that are strategically placed with explanation	John—Paper maché project with cities, parks, railroads, and so on that are created, labeled, and explained
Complex-thinking layer of learning	Rosita—Presentation of a written report that details many human features in the world (cities, parks, railroads, and so on)	Karla—Detailed drawing with accurate labels showing cities, parks, railroads, and so on that are strategically placed, with in-depth explanation	Daniel—Actual city map on which authentic features of the city (parks, railroads, and so on) are pinpointed

You can turn the project presentation into a meaningful learning experience for all students with a simple template such as the one in Table 4-7.

Table 4-7. Kinesthetic Project: Audience Participation Sheet

Participant Name: Helga Presenter Name: Daniel Project Uniquenesses: Daniel's project was really cool because we could see where all of the human features are in our own city.	Two interesting ideas that I learned about: 1) Our city has lots of parks that I didn't know about. 2) Our school is located almost right in the middle of the town.
What I'd like more information about is: 1) Where the movie theaters are in our city 2) Where all of the skate parks are	My visual reminder for the information that I learned looks like this: RIALTO MOVIES　CITY HALL　SAL'S PIZZA MAIN STREET SECOND AVENUE　Skate Park　PARK　THIRD AVENUE　SCHOOL PARK STREET LIBRARY

The project rubric shown in Table 4-8 takes into consideration students' content knowledge, the process used to develop the project, the final product, and the demonstration of knowledge through an oral report.

Table 4-8. Kinesthetic Project: Rubric

PERFORMANCE CRITERIA	3	2	1
Content: Topic, ideas, concepts, knowledge, and opinions demonstrate clear understanding of the curriculum standards.	Project reflects broad research and application of skills pertaining to topic, ideas, concepts, knowledge, and opinions with notable insight regarding the curriculum standards.	Project reflects some research and application of skills pertaining to topic, ideas, concepts, knowledge, and opinions with little insight regarding the curriculum standards.	Project reflects little or no research and application of skills pertaining to topic, ideas, concepts, knowledge, and opinions. Additional insights regarding curriculum standards are not evident.
Process: Project plan was followed using materials, timeline, collaboration, and research.	Project plan was followed using appropriate materials, an effective timeline, positive group collaboration, and extensive research.	Project plan was followed but was missing one or two of the following: appropriate materials, an effective timeline, positive group collaboration, or extensive research.	Project plan was not clearly followed and/ or was missing two or more of the following: appropriate materials, an effective timeline, positive group collaboration, or extensive research.
Product: Project clearly demonstrates content goals and expectations.	Project display clearly and effectively demonstrates assigned goals and expectations.	Project display demonstrates partial understanding of assigned goals and expectations.	Project display shows limited or no understanding of assigned goals and expectations.
Presentation: Presentation is sequential and clear, demonstrating in-depth knowledge of the topic.	Presentation is sequential and clear, demonstrating in-depth knowledge of the topic.	Presentation is somewhat sequential, demonstrating some knowledge of the topic.	Presentation is lacking a clear sequence, demonstrating little knowledge of the topic.

Student Journal Entries

Student journal entries are an effective and flexible instructional and assessment tool that can be used across the curriculum with any content standard or goal. Journals can be considered a performance assessment in that the learning is not just assessed but expanded and enhanced during the assessment. Additionally, it is an assessment that flows naturally from the instruction. There are hundreds of uses for and types of journal formats; we will focus only on those that we feel are most effectively used as performance assessments.

When should I use them? Choosing a journal as your assessment strategy is most effective when you want your students to do the following:

- Analyze experiences, solve problems, or consider varying perspectives.

- Examine or compare relationships with others and the world.

- Reflect on personal values, goals, and ideals.

- Summarize ideas, experiences, and opinions before and after instruction.

- Provide a thorough explanation to an open-ended question.

- Think beyond the essential knowledge layer of learning.

In addition, student journal entries will allow you to do the following:

- Compare current skills and knowledge with past skills and knowledge (by reading previous entries).

- Determine the depth of student understanding through written responses.

- View thinking strategies or problem-solving techniques students are using in their assignment tasks.

- Gain insights into students' opinions, experiences, goals, beliefs, and understandings of relationships.

- Foster written communication skills and self-expression.

- Enhance complex thinking through the modeling of your own writing.

To teach journaling, start with a prompt and work together to write a sample response. Students can copy the class response in their own journal or write one of their own. For example, if students are using journals during a literature study, project onto a screen the types of thoughts and questions that you want your students to use, such as "I wonder why the author gave us so much detailed information about the character's appearance" or "My prediction is that the other students will learn to like Leah even though she is so old-fashioned in her appearance." Then, with a chart, work together to write a sample response.

Scoring journal entries can sometimes present a problem. Scoring options depend upon the purpose for the writing and the type of journal assessment employed. For example, if your goal is to develop written fluency, student expression, vocabulary expansion, reflections, or comprehension, you wouldn't want to grade or correct the writing on the student's first attempt. Instead, comment on your students' writing or ask questions to promote deeper thinking. On the other hand, sometimes the journal—or part of it, such as an explanation of a math concept or a cause-and-effect entry about a historical event—is being used as a final assessment. In this case, you could easily grade the journal with a rubric. Whether you formally grade or informally assess, you should offer suggestions, constructive remarks, questions, and encouragement whenever possible. Encourage students from time to time to respond to your comments.

Double-Entry Journals

A double-entry journal allows students to compose and record two different responses. On the lefthand page of the notebook, the student writes one of the components (for example, *cause*), and on the right they record a corresponding response (for example, *effect*). Either side of the entry may include a comment, question, connection, analysis, reflection, or answer. Often, the teacher creates the "prompt," which is written on the left. Students then create the corresponding response on the right. Examples of double-entry journals are shown in Table 4-9 on page 86. What would you add to this list?

Table 4-9. Double-Entry Journal Writing

PROMPT → →	CONNECTION
Quote From Text "Well, the woman fell to talking about how hard times was, and how poor they had to live, and how the rats was as free as if they owned the place, and so forth and so on, and then I got easy again. She was right about the rats. You'd see one stick his nose out of a hole in the corner every little while. She said she had to have things handy to throw at them when she was alone, or they wouldn't give her no peace." Excerpt from *The Adventures of Huckleberry Finn*	Inferences or interpretations
Quote From Text "If someone loves a flower, of which just one single blossom grows in all the millions and millions of stars, it is enough to make him happy just to look at the stars. He can say to himself, 'Somewhere, my flower is there …' But if the sheep eats the flower, in one moment all his stars will be darkened … And you think that is not important!" Excerpt from *The Little Prince*	Connections to self or world
Quote From Text "Bee had made every effort to change herself this year. Tibby quietly suspected she knew the reason. Bee couldn't outrun her troubles, so she'd entered her own version of the witness protection program. Tibby knew how it was to lose someone you loved. And she also knew how tempting it was to cast off that sad, ruined part of yourself like a sweater you'd outgrown." Excerpt from *The Second Summer of the Sisterhood*	Student analysis of author's motivation or author's effectiveness
Essential Question Example: What are the similarities and differences between the American Revolution and the Civil War?	Connections or enhancement of other learned skills
Poem LOOK how the pale queen of the silent night Doth cause the ocean to attend upon her, And he, as long as she is in his sight, With her full tide is ready her to honor. Excerpt from *A Sonnet of the Moon*	

(continued)

Table 4-9. Double-Entry Journal Writing (continued)

PROMPT → →	CONNECTION
Posed Problem List the natural resources in your town that are most and least prominent. Which resources are lacking? Why are they needed? What avenues could you explore to develop these resources or bring them to your town? Use problem-solving steps to show your plan.	Posed solution to problem
Posed Math Problem John's parents give him $.50 per day for lunch. If John saves his lunch money for two weeks, how much money will he have?	Steps student will use to solve problem
Controversial Topic or Concept World population: Is the world overpopulated? If so, what steps should we be taking? If not, how do we manage the growth rates? Share your thoughts, beliefs, and feelings about this topic.	Emotional reactions
Controversial Topic or Concept Are the world's rainforests really being depleted? Research this topic and form your opinion based on your findings.	Formulation of viewpoint based on experience, opinion, and research
Term and Definition Calculation: Careful, often cunning estimation and planning of likely outcomes, especially to advance one's own interests.	Symbol, sketch, or other visual demonstration
Term With Student Prediction Based on Background Knowledge Term: Disregard Sample student response: I know "dis" means not and I think "regard" means having respect for something. So I'm going to predict that disregard means not having respect for something.	Actual term definition after looking in dictionary or glossary
Quotes From Text That Student Found Puzzling or Intriguing "I'm not what I once was, and neither, by the end, was he. The geese are making a mess of the pond, and the yellow Lab gets to run every morning with her master. The first couple of times she was walked by herself were particularly sad. Bea misses Beau terribly, I suspect, but I may just be projecting again." Excerpt from *Good Dog, Stay*	Reactions, ideas, questions

(continued)

Table 4-9. Double-Entry Journal Writing (continued)

PROMPT → →	CONNECTION
Open-Ended Question What causes a star to collapse?	"I wonder" statements
Math Problem With Student Answer Sample student problem: 3/5 = 6/10 = 0.6	Reflections about strategies used to solve problem
Science Experiment: Checklist or Steps That Student Will Follow When Conducting the Experiment 1. Ask a question. 2. Do background research. 3. Construct a hypothesis. 4. Test your hypothesis by doing an experiment. 5. Analyze your data and draw a conclusion. 6. Communicate your results.	Reflections, self-assessment, or new learning that resulted from the experiment
Historical Event Sample event: The assassination of John F. Kennedy	Comparisons to another historical event
Reflections on a Project or Assignment Sample student response: I think my persuasive essay about the death penalty was convincing and relied heavily on emotional appeal techniques.	What student will do differently on a similar task

Student Self-Assessment

If our goal is to develop complex and strategic thinking in our students, as well as self-reliant and active learners, then we must involve students directly in the *process* of learning. Student self-assessment involves consistent opportunities for learners to reflect on the quality of their learning, evaluate their strengths and weaknesses, and create plans for altering or modifying their learning strategies.

Self-assessment can take a number of forms:

- Discussions—partner groups, larger groups, or whole class
- Learning or reflection journals

- Self-assessment checklists
- Rubric evaluations
- Writing conferences
- Teacher-student conferences
- Graphic organizers

When should I use it? Prior to beginning any assignment, project, or task, give students a clear understanding of the performance criteria. They are much more likely to become academically successful if they know in advance what is expected of them. As students evaluate their own work, they can review the performance criteria and compare their work to each of its components. When this type of interaction with the evaluation process becomes routine, students quickly learn the importance of adhering to the criteria, begin taking more responsibility for their work, and gain proficiency in judging its quality.

You too will gain new perspectives from student self-assessment. Student observations and reflections provide constructive feedback that may inspire you to alter your instructional plan. And of course, as you read student self-assessment journals or listen to discussions, you gain a better picture of whether they are really learning what you are teaching. Let's take a look at several sample student self-assessment tools.

Self-Assessment #1

Success Gauge: Students fill in the arrow in Figures 4-4 and 4-5 on page 90 that shows their level of understanding and how well they used thinking strategies.

Self-Assessment #2

In this tool, shown in Table 4-10 on page 91, students rate themselves and then justify their thinking.

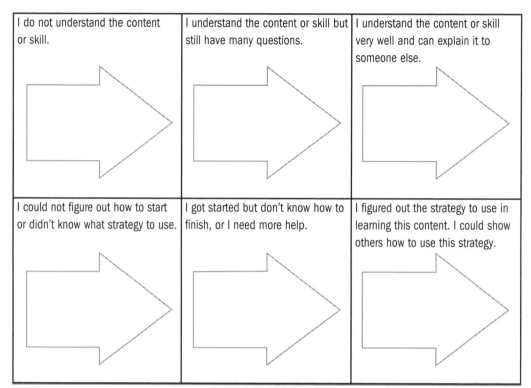

I do not understand the content or skill.	I understand the content or skill but still have many questions.	I understand the content or skill very well and can explain it to someone else.
I could not figure out how to start or didn't know what strategy to use.	I got started but don't know how to finish, or I need more help.	I figured out the strategy to use in learning this content. I could show others how to use this strategy.

Figure 4-4. Success Gauge: Understanding

Tell what you might try differently when you next do an assignment like this one.

How could you be more successful?

_____

What new strategies might you try?

_____

Figure 4-5. Success Gauge: Strategies/Thinking Skills

Table 4–10. Student Self-Rating

	YOUR RATING	YOUR EXPLANATION
4. Expert Eggbert	X	I understand how to divide a 3- digit number by a 2-digit number, and I helped some of the people at my table who didn't get it.
3. Smarty Pants		
2. Learning Larry		
1. Newbie		

Scale:
4 = Expert level; know it and can explain it
3 = Know it well; will progress to expert level soon
2 = Learning it but need more time to become a smarty pants
1 = Starting fresh as a newbie with this learning; need lots of practice

Selected-Response Quiz

A selected-response assessment can be in a multiple-choice, fill-in-the-blank, true/false, or matching format. This type of assessment is efficient and can be scored quickly. Each question has a right and wrong answer, and the scoring is unbiased.

When should I use it? Selected-response assessment is appropriate when testing basic knowledge or understanding, essential skills, or simple processes. It is not as effective when testing higher order skills such as reasoning, judging, or analyzing.

Summative Assessment

Thinking back to the terminology section from chapter 1, you know that a summative assessment is a test or measurement of achievement usually given at the end of a unit, course, or program to judge student proficiency. We usually think of summative assessments as being in a selected-response format, such as semester exams or standardized norm-referenced tests. But they also should frequently be performance-based, in the form of a research paper or oral presentation.

Taken literally, summative assessment means that students have one shot at being successful—truly a sink-or-swim mentality. Think back to your college days when you took classes that did not assess your understanding throughout the semester, but rather relied on one midterm and one final exam. Most were in a selected-response format, and if this format didn't happen to be a learning style that made sense to you, you were out of luck. Educators are now rethinking the role of assessment, because we have gained so much knowledge about how the brain processes information and how individual and unique is each person's way of demonstrating that information. However, standardized testing such as state tests, district tests, and college entrance exams still exists, and we have to help our students to prepare for summative assessments by teaching them test-taking strategies and tips. For this reason, even if preparation time and class time weren't a factor, we should still occasionally use selected-response formats in conjunction with our performance assessments.

There are two major types of summative assessments:

- **Norm-referenced assessments** compare all test-takers to each other and are measured with a "curve" to demonstrate level of proficiency. They are usually composed of selected-response items. Examples include final semester exams, statewide standardized tests, and college entrance exams (for example, SATs).

- **Criterion-referenced assessments** measure achievement based on a predetermined standard or set of criteria. Criterion-referenced tests can be teacher-made, provided by the district, or from a textbook. Give your students the expected criteria when the target is introduced, so that they are aware of the expectations.

Because each student best demonstrates new knowledge in a unique way, we recommend that an end-of-lesson or end-of-unit assessment integrate a performance assessment with a short, selected-response assessment. As always, when student final products are a natural result of the learning, they are much more relevant and meaningful to a student.

Thinking About Your Thinking

For assessment to be truly focused, it must involve multiple tasks, activities, formats, and designs for evaluating the progress and accomplishments of students throughout the learning cycle.

A *preassessment* can show current understanding and helps the student and teacher determine where the learning needs to start. Pretests may take the form of a journal entry, a multiple-choice format, a concept map, an oral discussion, or teacher questioning.

Informal assessments are the measurement of how well students are progressing *as* the learning is taking place. This could entail teacher observation with checklists, cooperative group sharing, journal entries, practice assignments from the text, or a variety of other informal tasks. When translating rubric scores and percentages into grades at the end of the unit, pretests and informal assessments should not be included.

When students have had extensive instruction and practice, they demonstrate their new understandings through *growth assessments*. Although they are still learning, they have had enough exposure to the material that the teacher may feel comfortable including the data from growth assessments in the final profile. Growth assessments might take the form of 3-minute talks, essays, kinesthetic projects, or graphic representations.

One very effective way to showcase the multiple efforts that students have displayed throughout their learning is through a final showing of their activities. We suggest asking all students to use a three-piece project board (similar to those used for science projects) that can be folded and stored when not in use. At the end of a unit, students are given back all of their assessment activities to post on their boards. (Using staples or thumbtacks, rather than glue or tape, enables them to use the board multiple times.) Ask students to write a summary of their learning or to do an oral presentation with the project board as their visual. The project board and presentation could then serve as the *final student product*.

Tools and Templates

The tools in this section can also be found online at teachinginfocus.com.

Tool 10: Checklist

Using this tool, assess during the learning process whether or not students have met the expectations of the learning. Content standards or goals are listed in column 1. The process by which students will meet the expectations of the standard is listed alongside it.

	CONTENT EXPECTATIONS	PROCESS EXPECTATIONS	YES/NO WITH DATES
Student #1	Assessment #1		
	Assessment #2		
	Assessment #3		
Student #2	Assessment #1		
	Assessment #2		
	Assessment #3		

Tool 11: SQ3R Organizer

SQ3R stands for *Survey, Question, Read, Recite,* and *Review.* This graphic organizer spans the entire lesson—beginning, middle, and end, and is extremely effective during the reading of nonfiction text.

Name _____

Topic or Story Title:			
SURVEY	**QUESTION**	**READ**	**RECITE**
Record important titles and subtitles from chapter sections.	Write who, what, when, where, and why questions for the main topics and subtopics.	After reading, write answers to the five questions that were written.	Record additional interesting facts related to the five questions to complement the information that was discovered during the reading.

Review: On the reverse side, compose a one-paragraph summary for each of the questions that were answered. Use this as a study guide.

Tool 12: Student Organizer

Semantic Feature Analysis

Student Directions: To review a group of concepts, fill in the boxes below with a "+" if the concept is associated with the attribute and a "−" if the concept is not associated with the attribute.

CONCEPT	ATTRIBUTES			
		→	→	

Tool 13: Three-Minute Talk

The use of a 3-minute talk when combined with visual representations that the student has created is a highly effective assessment practice for the essential knowledge, application, and complex-thinking layers.

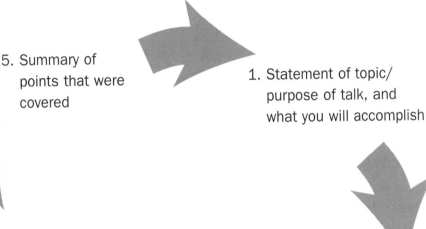

5. Summary of points that were covered

1. Statement of topic/ purpose of talk, and what you will accomplish

4. Clear statement of third point with rationale or reasons

2. Clear statement of first point with rationale or reasons

3. Clear statement of second point with rationale or reasons

Tool 14: Three-Minute Talk Performance Criteria

Providing a rubric at the beginning of instruction informs students about the final expectations for the learning. (*What exactly are we going to be held accountable for knowing and doing?*) A simple differentiation tactic for the 3-minute talk would involve two or three graphic organizers tailored for the essential knowledge, application, and complex-thinking layers of learning.

ESSENTIAL KNOWLEDGE	APPLICATION	COMPLEX THINKING
Main ideas are accurately presented.	Main ideas are accurately presented with speaker's own ideas, inferences, or conclusions based on the content.	Main ideas are accurately presented and merged with speaker's own ideas, judgment, or conclusions based on the content.
Supporting details explain the main ideas in logical and sequential form.	Supporting details explain and clarify the main ideas in logical and sequential form.	Supporting details explain, clarify, and elaborate on the main ideas in logical and sequential form.
There is a clear introduction, an organized body with at least two main ideas, and a clear closure.	There is a clear introduction, an organized body with at least three main ideas, and a clear closure.	There is a creative and clear introduction, an organized and articulate body with at least three main ideas, and a clear closure.
The vocabulary is appropriate to both the content and the audience.	The vocabulary is appropriate to both the content and the audience. Speaker takes time to explain content-specific terms.	The vocabulary is appropriate to both the content and the audience. Speaker appropriately uses and explains content-specific terms.
Student-created visuals such as pictures, diagrams, computer-generated products, videos, and other tools are used appropriately to support the presentation.	Student-created visuals such as pictures, diagrams, computer-generated products, videos, and other tools are used effectively to support the presentation.	Speaker devises techniques to engage the audience and hold their interest. Student-created visuals such as pictures, diagrams, computer-generated products, videos, and other tools are used effectively to support the presentation.
Voice quality (pitch, rate, volume) is minimally sufficient.	Voice quality (pitch, rate, volume) is adequate.	Voice quality (pitch, rate, volume) is proficient.
Speaker uses eye contact and gestures appropriately.	Speaker uses eye contact and gestures appropriately.	Speaker uses eye contact and gestures appropriately.
Speaker interacts with audience and answers questions.	Speaker interacts with audience and answers questions with insightful responses.	Speaker interacts with audience and answers questions with insightful responses.

Tool 15: Student-Choice Projects

Learning Target: _____

Student Names and Project Description			
	AUDITORY PROJECT	VISUAL PROJECT	KINESTHETIC PROJECT
Essential knowledge layer of learning			
Application layer of learning			
Complex-thinking layer of learning			

Tool 16: Student-Choice Project Participation Sheet

Student directions: Use this template to provide feedback to other students about their project presentations.

KINESTHETIC PROJECT: AUDIENCE PARTICIPATION SHEET	
Participant Name: Presenter Name: Project Uniquenesses:	Two interesting ideas that I learned about: 1) 2)
What I'd like more information about is: 1) 2)	My visual reminder for the information that I learned looks like this:

Tool 17: Success Gauge

Student Directions: Fill in the arrow that shows your level of understanding and how well you used thinking strategies.

Understanding Learning Target: _____

_____

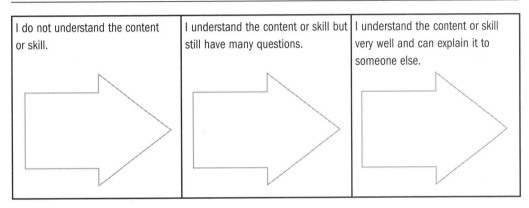

| I do not understand the content or skill. | I understand the content or skill but still have many questions. | I understand the content or skill very well and can explain it to someone else. |

Strategies/Thinking Skills Learning Target: _____

_____

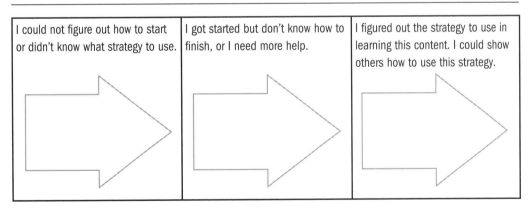

| I could not figure out how to start or didn't know what strategy to use. | I got started but don't know how to finish, or I need more help. | I figured out the strategy to use in learning this content. I could show others how to use this strategy. |

Tell what you might try differently when you next do an assignment like this one. How could you be more successful? What new strategies might you try?

_____

_____

Tool 18: Self-Assessment Rating

Student Directions: Rate yourself and then justify your decision.

Scale:

4 = Expert level; know it and can explain it

3 = Know it well; will progress to expert level soon

2 = Learning it but need more time to become a smarty pants

1 = Starting fresh as a newbie with this learning; need lots of practice

Learning Target: _____

_____

	YOUR RATING	YOUR EXPLANATION
4. Expert Eggbert		
3. Smarty Pants		
2. Learning Larry		
1. Newbie		

Customizing the Assessment

The artistry of classroom assessment emerges when teachers orchestrate a careful alignment among user information needs, achievement targets, and assessment methods.

—Rick Stiggins

In this chapter . . .

- Thinking About Assessment
- Ms. Rumon's Third-Grade Classroom
- Thinking About Your Thinking
- Tools and Templates

Thinking About Assessment

As we have seen, in making decisions about which assessment format works best for the content standard that you are teaching, you need to take into consideration the diverse learners in your classroom. Most likely, the assessment format you choose will have to be altered or customized to meet their various needs. Remember that while at first some students will exceed the expectations of the standard you are teaching and some may take longer to reach it, all must meet the expectations of the standard as it is written. Having selected the type of assessment you wish to use, what changes can you make in it so that all students are demonstrating their knowledge at the level for which they are ready? Let's look at how Ms. Rumon differentiated an assessment for her elementary students.

Ms. Rumon's Third-Grade Classroom

Ms. Rumon is creating a social studies unit on famous Americans. She starts by choosing one of the standards she will teach:

 Students will correctly sequence historical data about famous Americans to create an accurate timeline.

Because she is familiar with the layers of learning, she knows this standard is at the application layer of learning. To meet it, students already need to know what a timeline is and what it does. She inserts a pretest into her unit plan that *preassesses* how well students understand that a timeline shows a sequence of historical events. The preassessment also checks to see if students already know the content goal or standard.

Next, Ms. Rumon wants to ensure that students who do not perform well on the pretest have additional instruction at the essential knowledge layer before she instructs them at the application layer. For these students, she customizes the learning by developing a method for assessing student proficiency after she has taught the essential knowledge understanding of what a timeline is and does.

For gifted students and high achievers, Ms. Rumon customizes the learning so they are more challenged. To do this, she develops a method for assessing student proficiency at the complex-thinking layer. For grading purposes, these higher-achieving students will not be held accountable for achievement beyond the standard expectations (application level), but she will provide learning and achievement opportunities beyond that level.

Layers of Learning for Assessment

Content assessment items should be specific to the three different content expectations (essential knowledge, application, and complex thinking) and based on student readiness. Ms. Rumon may either assign the same assessment format (for example, an oral report, essay, journal entry, poster, or diorama) to *all* students, or she may allow students to choose their own formative assessment format. If she chooses the latter, she will need to provide a specific planning sheet with a timeline to which they should adhere. In either case, each of the three layers of learning will have its own rubric based on content expectations, as shown in Tables 5-1 (below) and 5-2 (page 106). Students will revisit the learning rubric to ensure that they are demonstrating the required knowledge expectations.

 Students will correctly sequence historical data about famous Americans to create an accurate timeline.

Table 5-1. Performance Criteria for the Three Layers of Learning

LAYERS OF LEARNING	PERFORMANCE CRITERIA FOR THREE LAYERS
Essential Knowledge	Performance Criteria: Students will *understand* that a timeline can demonstrate the sequence of historical events of famous Americans. They will have a general understanding of life events of three famous Americans.
Application	Performance Criteria: Students will correctly *sequence* historical data of famous Americans to create an accurate timeline. They will have a detailed understanding of the life events of four famous Americans.
Complex Thinking	Performance Criteria: Students will *create* and *interpret* historical timelines, and *make judgments about* the life events of four or more famous Americans.

Ms. Rumon has analyzed the standard and knows that it is written in the application layer. She knows that the two main skills involved are sequencing historical data in a timeline format and learning about famous Americans. She will now determine how to customize the assessment formats to meet the readiness levels of her students.

Table 5-2. Rubric: Historical Data Timeline

PERFORMANCE CRITERIA	3	2	1
Essential Knowledge Performance Criteria: Students will *understand* that a timeline can demonstrate the sequence of historical events of famous Americans. They will have an understanding of life events of three famous Americans.	Student journal explanations, oral group discussion, and creation of historical timeline events clearly demonstrate a thorough understanding of timeline concepts and purposes. Understanding of three famous Americans' events is evident.	Student journal explanations, oral group discussion, and creation of historical timeline events demonstrate a fair understanding of timeline concepts and purposes. Understanding of famous Americans' events is not completely evident.	Student journal explanations, oral group discussion, and creation of historical timeline events demonstrate little or no understanding of timeline concepts and purposes. Understanding of famous Americans' events is not evident.
Application Performance Criteria: Students will correctly sequence historical data of famous Americans to create an accurate timeline. They will understand life events of four famous Americans.	Graphic organizer to sequence data and final timeline product demonstrate an accurate and well-planned timeline. Understanding of life events of four Americans is demonstrated clearly.	Graphic organizer to sequence data and final timeline product demonstrate a somewhat accurate, somewhat planned timeline. Understanding of life events of four Americans is demonstrated to a fair degree.	Graphic organizer to sequence data and final timeline product demonstrate a less-than-accurate timeline with little evidence of planning. Understanding of life events of four Americans is not evident.
Complex Thinking Performance Criteria: Students will *create* and *interpret* historical timelines, and *make judgments about* the life events of four or more famous Americans.	Graphic organizer to interpret the timeline, planning sheet to transfer information to a project, and final project demonstrate an accurate interpretation and high level of critical thinking skills. Student shows sound reasoning in judgments that are made regarding famous Americans.	Graphic organizer to interpret the timeline, planning sheet to transfer information to a project, and final project demonstrate a somewhat accurate interpretation with some evidence of critical thinking. Student shows some reasoning in judgments that are made regarding famous Americans.	Graphic organizer to interpret the timeline, planning sheet to transfer information to a project, and final project demonstrate little accuracy of interpretation with little or no evidence of critical thinking. Student shows little or no reasoning in judgments that are made regarding famous Americans.

Preassessment With Customization

Preassessment #1: Questionnaire. In the preassessment, students will fill out a questionnaire like the one shown in Table 5-3 to show what they already know about the upcoming topic.

Table 5-3. Preassessment Questionnaire

Name: Linda McCarthy Date: March 18	Skill: Students will correctly sequence historical data about famous Americans to create an accurate timeline.
Some of the famous Americans that I know something about are . . .	George Washington, Abe Lincoln
The famous Americans that I would like to learn about are . . .	Hillary Clinton, Britney Spears
An example of a **sequence** would be . . .	Something that's in order??
What the phrase **historical data** means to me is . . .	I'm not sure—historical means that it was a long time ago.
What I know about a **timeline** is that . . .	It's a line with numbers on it.
If I were to draw a timeline of my day yesterday, it would look like this . . .	I'm not sure how to do this.

Customization. Ms. Rumon will work in a small group with English-language learners and other students who may not be able to participate in a written preassessment. Instead of assessing their reading proficiency, she will ask questions orally and use visuals in order to determine their readiness for the specific learning target.

Preassessment #2: Term Cards. She will pass out a 3 x 5 card to each student and have them copy the words *timeline, historical, data,* and *sequence* on both the front and back. On the front of the card, she will ask them to tell everything that they know about those words. Students will then engage in a discussion about the actual meanings of these terms. Later, as they learn more about the words, they will fill out the backs of the cards with additional information. They can also use their journals to explain vocabulary understanding and how it relates to the content. This activity will determine their current understanding of vocabulary words that will be crucial as they sequence a timeline using historical data.

Customization. English-language learners or students who are not proficient with reading and writing may work with a partner to complete the activity. Another customization could be to ask students to be responsible for defining two of the four words or to create visual depictions of the word meanings. Eventually these students will be expected to become proficient with all four words.

Informal Assessment With Customization

Especially in the beginning stages of learning, teachers need multiple opportunities, including informal ones, to monitor student understanding.

Informal Assessment #1: Show What You Know. This can be used throughout instruction to assess current student understanding. At certain intervals, Ms. Rumon could assign a quick question or task. Students could write down the answer on their paper and hold it up in the air while she takes a quick walk around the room to assess their understanding. This is also a time that she could make observations about body language and facial expressions.

Customization. If students look confused or look at answers other students are holding up before writing on their own paper, that will be a signal to Ms. Rumon that reteaching for these students may be in order. Another customization involves questions or tasks that are at a slightly more—or less—difficult level:

- Draw a timeline with three events.

- Draw a timeline with three events in correct sequential order.

- Draw a timeline with three historical events in correct sequential order.

Informal Assessment #2: Partner Choices. At certain intervals throughout instruction, Ms. Rumon will project multiple-choice questions onto a screen or write them on a whiteboard. She will ask students to work with a partner to choose A, B, C, or D as the best answer. As partners discuss which answer is best, she will walk around the room listening to determine understanding levels. Next, she will share the correct answer and explain why it is correct before moving on with the lesson. Each partner multiple-choice segment should take no more than 3 to 4 minutes.

Customization: Ms. Rumon will use two or three different multiple-choice question options with varying degrees of difficulty for each of these segments.

Growth Assessment With Customization

As students gain more skill and higher levels of understanding, she will use growth assessments to measure degrees of learning. These may often be in the form of performance tasks that use a rubric for scoring.

Growth Assessment #1: Check What You Know. Ms. Rumon will give students tools, such as graphic organizers, to demonstrate their knowledge. The organizers in Tables 5-4 to 5-6 on pages 109–110 would be effective for students to use in showing their knowledge of famous Americans they have been studying.

Table 5-4. Customization: Essential Knowledge Layer of Learning

	MARTIN LUTHER KING, JR.	SUSAN B. ANTHONY	HELEN KELLER
Known for . . .			
What you found most interesting			

Table 5-5. Customization: Application Layer of Learning

	MARTIN LUTHER KING, JR.	SUSAN B. ANTHONY	HELEN KELLER	JACKIE ROBINSON
Known for . . .				
Outstanding attributes				
What you found most interesting				
What you'd like to know more about				

Table 5-6. Customization: Complex-Thinking Layer of Learning

	MARTIN LUTHER KING, JR.	SUSAN B. ANTHONY	HELEN KELLER	JACKIE ROBINSON
Known for . . .				
Outstanding attributes				
What you found most interesting				
What you'd like to know more about				
What are your feelings or judgments (Short answer)				

Growth Assessment #2: Historical Comic Strips. As students gain more skill and higher levels of understanding, growth assessments can measure the progress of their learning. These growth assessments often consist of performance tasks that use a rubric for scoring.

In "Historical Comic Strips," students will be asked to choose one of the famous Americans that they have been studying and place the important events of that person's life in chronological order, using pictures and dialogue in comic-strip frames.

Customization: Ms. Rumon will give some students a comic-strip template with fewer frames to fill in. She will give higher-achieving students a template with a greater number of frames.

Final Student Product

This can be an accumulation of learning tasks or a single comprehensive task that demonstrates the depth of student understanding of the goal.

Final Student Product #1: Poster-Board Timeline. To demonstrate learning of the content standard, students will use a poster board to create a detailed timeline, clearly and neatly constructed with color and detail, that shows the following:

- Important personal and political events in the lives of at least three famous Americans

- Events listed in a sequential order, from earliest to latest

- A timeline constructed with equal segments of time

Customization. Students in the essential knowledge layer of learning will only be responsible for basic events and timeline construction for three famous Americans. Students in the application layer should demonstrate an accurate and detailed timeline showing the events of four famous Americans. Students in the complex-thinking layer of learning will demonstrate an accurate and detailed timeline showing the events of four famous Americans. In addition, they will make judgments about which American contributed the most to their country.

Final Student Product #2: Three-Minute Talk. Students will present a 3-minute talk to share the events of a famous American they have selected. A visual—the completed timelines—should accompany the presentation, in which students will do the following:

1. State the topic and purpose of the talk, and what they will accomplish.

2. Give a clear statement of the first life event with rationale or reasons.

3. Give a clear statement of a second life event with the reason for choosing it.

4. Give a clear statement of the third life event with rationale or reasons.

5. Give a summary of the important events that were covered.

Customization. Students can have different expectations regarding the number of events they discuss. Complex-thinking-layer students might be expected to share their decisions about which American contributed most to the United States.

Whatever layer of learning a student starts with, all need exposure to ongoing assessment with focused feedback through a variety of formats and designs. As you begin making informed assessment decisions, consider implementing both performance and selected-response formats into your lessons. Students are expected to be proficient in selected-response assessment formats for state and local summative assessments, and they need opportunities to learn these test-taking skills. An example of this combination might take the shape of a 5-paragraph essay plus 10 multiple-choice items, or a 3-minute oral presentation, 5 fill-in-the-blank questions, and 5 matching questions.

Thinking About Your Thinking

This chapter has emphasized the importance of customizing your assessments. An important aspect of customization involves analyzing a standard and creating assessment expectations for the three layers of learning. In Table 5-7, share your thoughts about the importance of customizing the assessment. In the left column, rank the importance of each statement with regard to assessment, with 5 being extremely important and 1 being completely irrelevant or unimportant.

Table 5-7. Customization Poll

MY RANKING	MY REASONS FOR THIS RANKING
Creating three layers of assessments (essential knowledge, application, and complex thinking) makes sense to me. 1 2 3 4 5	
Analyzing a standard gives me, the teacher, a clearer understanding of the depth to which students need to understand the content or skills. 1 2 3 4 5	
Customizing each assessment so that there are three layers will help meet the needs of students at different readiness levels. 1 2 3 4 5	
All students should be expected to eventually meet the expectations of the standard as it is written, but not all students will get there at the same time. 1 2 3 4 5	
It makes sense to create a combination of a performance assessment with a selected-response format in my lesson. 1 2 3 4 5	

Tools and Templates

The tools in this section can also be found online at teachinginfocus.com.

Tool 19: Customizing the Assessment

Look at the content standard in the table below. Seeing the verb *describe,* we know that this expectation is in the application layer of learning. In the empty boxes, create a content expectation for students who are not yet ready for this layer and a content expectation for students who have already demonstrated proficiency with this standard.

LAYER OF LEARNING	CUSTOMIZED EXPECTATIONS
Essential Knowledge: (Not yet ready for the application layer of learning)	
Application:	**Content Standard:** Describe the author's use of literary elements (for example, characterization, setting, plot, and theme).
Complex Thinking: (Has demonstrated proficiency at the application layer)	

What type of assessment would you envision for this content standard?

_____

_____

_____

_____

_____

_____

_____

Tool 20: Preassessment

Student Directions: Fill out a questionnaire to show what you already know about the upcoming topic.

Name: Date:	Skill:
Questions or prompts:	**Student response prior to instruction:**

Customization. Work in a small group with English-language learners and other students who may not be able to participate in a written preassessment. Instead of assessing their reading proficiency, go through the questions orally in order to determine students' readiness for the specific learning target. Use visuals and examples for students who are not fluent with the English language.

Tool 21: Rubric for Customized Assessment

Content Standard(s):

_____

_____

PERFORMANCE CRITERIA ↓	3	2	1
Essential Knowledge:			
Application:			
Complex Thinking:			

Creating a Unit Assessment Plan

If we align our class assessments with our class goals, then when students work toward one, they will naturally be working toward the other.

—Jeffrey K. Smith, Lisa F. Smith, and Richard De Lisi

In this chapter . . .

- Thinking About Assessment
- Building the Unit Assessment Plan
- Thinking About Your Thinking
- Tools and Templates

Thinking About Assessment

In addition to assessments that will be scored, you will most likely be asking questions, observing, and providing other informal assessments throughout the instructional process to determine the status of knowledge relating to the standard being taught. Although they are informal, these assessments should be designed to provide an accurate picture of current student knowledge. For example, maybe you currently use the "thumbs up if you understand" method. While this is certainly a quick and easy way to make sure students are awake and paying attention, it does not really ensure that they had the foggiest notion of what you were talking about. A more precise informal assessment in this case might be to periodically ask students to be ready to share one new piece of learning with the class. This brings their level of concern up a notch, and they will feel more accountable for listening if they know you have a few surprises planned. Give them 1 minute to either reread the content or discuss it with a partner. At the end of 1 minute, you may call on only one student to share the new learning, but all students will have been preparing. We have always viewed techniques like this as an instructional strategy, but they are also a means by which to assess student understanding.

Building the Unit Assessment Plan

When building a unit assessment, discussions with colleagues can provide important insights into better methods. An ongoing dialogue with your peers may not only be insightful, it may also show you new ways to keep students on task, tips for creating an environment in which all students feel responsible for the learning, and ways to better honor learning styles. There is never a downside to brainstorming and sharing assessment ideas and strategies with colleagues. Whether you are working in collaboration with other teachers or on your own to create a plan, this chapter will be helpful in taking you step by step through the process of building a focused assessment for a full unit. We will first demonstrate this process through the use of a fictional team of teachers from Pleasantdale Elementary as they undertake to do the following:

1. Determine focus standards based on the accumulated data they have reviewed.

2. Narrow down their standards of concern to the *one* goal they want to tackle first.

3. Analyze the standard to determine exactly what the learner needs to be able to know or do by the end of the unit or lesson.

4. Choose the terms and concepts related to the standard to ensure that both students and teachers are fluent in the common language.

5. Discuss with each other the performance criteria, rubrics, and selected-response formats to decide how they will assess the goals of the standard.

6. Use strategies for layers of learning and the assessment design grid to determine how to prioritize and best assess the goals of the standard.

7. Create the assessments—preassessment, informal assessment, growth assessment, and final student product.

8. Evaluate the effectiveness of the assessment prior to implementation.

Pleasantdale Elementary

The Team

- Don Ryan, fifth-grade teacher
- Jim Payne, fifth-grade teacher
- Laurie Richardson, teacher of English-language learners
- Lu Sabino, fifth-grade teacher
- Mardell Moreno, fifth-grade teacher

Don, Jim, Lu, and Mardell agreed that they would meet the week prior to the beginning of the school year in order to begin addressing some of the academic areas of concern. They invited Laurie to join the group because of the high percentage of ELLs and culturally diverse students in this year's fifth grade.

First Meeting: Developing Expectations and Goals

In their first meeting, the teachers decided to make sure they were all on the same page regarding each others' expectations and needs. To gain a clear understanding of their main goals and priorities regarding assessment, they asked these questions:

- Where do we want to go, and how are we going to get there? Will our plan be based on state standards, school goals, or district goals?
- What do we want students to learn—by grade level, course, and unit?
- How will we know when each student has acquired the knowledge and skills that we have taught?
- What will we do to prevent students from becoming frustrated when they experience initial difficulty in the learning?
- What will we do when preassessments show that they already know it?

The group decided that they wanted to determine the three areas of reading and math in which the most students were performing below grade level. Their goal was to bring students to a significantly higher level of achievement in those three areas. The final student product, along with the informal and growth assessments, would give them a comprehensive picture of student skill level. They also decided that they would challenge students who already knew the standard and scaffold the learning for students who weren't quite ready to undertake the standard as it was written.

Each teacher made a commitment to analyze prior assessment data on incoming fifth-graders to determine major areas of performance below grade level. They were each to look at the areas of reading and math that were most deficient and bring their findings back to the group. They determined that at the next meeting, they would narrow that list to the top three areas of concern that would be the focus for the school year.

Second Meeting: Choosing an Area of Focus

In the second meeting, each teacher was asked to report on findings regarding the areas of reading and math that were of highest priority. After much discussion and review of data, they narrowed down the highest needs to the three standards shown in Tables 6-1 to 6-3 on pages 120–121.

Table 6-1. Math Concept 1: Data Analysis (Statistics)

 Understand and apply data collection, organization, and representation to analyze and sort data.

PO 1. Formulate questions to collect data in contextual situations.
PO 2. Construct a histogram, line graph, scatter plot, or stem-and-leaf plot with appropriate labels and title from organized data.
PO 3. Interpret graphical representations and data displays including bar graphs (including double-bar), circle graphs, frequency tables, three-set Venn diagrams, and line graphs that display continuous data.
PO 4. Answer questions based on graphical representations, and data displays including bar graphs (including double-bar), circle graphs, frequency tables, three-set Venn diagrams, and line graphs that display continuous data.
PO 5. Identify the mode(s) and mean (average) of given data.
PO 6. Formulate reasonable predictions from a given set of data.
PO 7. Compare two sets of data related to the same investigation.
PO 8. Solve contextual problems using graphs, charts, and tables.

Table 6-2. Math Concept 1: Number Sense

 Understand and apply numbers, ways of representing numbers, the relationships among numbers, and different number systems.

PO 1. Make models that represent improper fractions.
PO 2. Identify symbols, words, or models that represent improper fractions.
PO 3. Use improper fractions in contextual situations.
PO 4. Compare two proper fractions or improper fractions with like denominators.
PO 5. Order 3 or more unit fractions, proper or improper fractions with like denominators, or mixed numbers with like denominators.
PO 6. Compare two whole numbers, fractions, and decimals (for example, 1/2 to 0.6).
PO 7. Order whole numbers, fractions, and decimals.
PO 8. Determine the equivalence between and among fractions, decimals, and percents in contextual situations.
PO 9. Identify all whole number factors and pairs of factors for a number.
PO 10. Recognize that 1 is neither a prime nor a composite number.
PO 11. Sort whole numbers (through 50) into sets containing only prime numbers or only composite numbers.

Table 6-3. Comprehension Performance Objectives

 Strand 1: Reading Process (Grade 5)

Use reading strategies (for example, drawing conclusions, determining cause and effect, making inferences, sequencing) to comprehend text.

PO 1. Use reading strategies to draw conclusions for reading comprehension.
PO 2. Use reading strategies to determine cause and effect for reading comprehension.
PO 3. Use reading strategies to make inferences in reading comprehension.
PO 4. Use reading strategies to sequence in reading comprehension.

Now that the team had chosen the three areas of most concern, they needed to decide which was the highest priority, so that they could get started with the development of a focused assessment for a full unit. Based on the standardized tests that were given to these students as fourth graders, they determined that comprehension strategies were the number-one area of immediate concern. Moreover, one of the district goals for the school year emphasized the use of student reading strategies, so the team now felt even more confident that this was the best choice for their first common assessment.

Because students were currently studying early Native Americans in their Social Studies course, teachers chose the novel *The Sign of the Beaver,* by Elizabeth George Speare, as the vehicle for teaching reading comprehension strategies. This literature study would foster more relevance and meaning for students because of the integration of two content areas.

Third Meeting: Analyzing the Standard

The sole mission of this meeting was to analyze the standard to ensure that each member was clear on exactly what students were expected to know or be able to do. Their reasoning was that before they could make sound decisions about instructional or assessment strategies, they all needed to feel secure about the end goal.

They decided to use essential knowledge, application, and complex-thinking layers of learning to determine the level of difficulty that students were expected to achieve. They began by writing the standard on a flip chart:

Use reading strategies (for example, drawing conclusions, determining cause and effect, making inferences, sequencing) to comprehend text.

They knew that less active verbs such as *know, understand,* or *identify* indicate essential knowledge or understanding; that standards asking students to apply their knowledge contain more active verbs such as *write, read, determine, sequence,* or *decide;* and that the third layer of learning expects students to use complex-thinking skills and typically contains verbs such as *analyze, synthesize, self-assess,* and *make judgments.* They next underlined the verbs in the standard:

Use reading strategies (for example, drawing conclusions, determining cause and effect, making inferences, sequencing) to comprehend text.

Because it was obvious that students were expected to do much more than know, understand, or identify, they immediately ruled out the essential knowledge layer of learning. They saw that students were expected to achieve at least the application layer of learning and possibly the complex-thinking layer. After much discussion, they agreed to label this standard a high level of application.

Next, they asked these important questions:

- What do we want students to learn?

- How will we know if they learned it?

- What will we do if they don't learn it?

- What will we do if they already know it?

(DuFour, DuFour, Eaker, & Many, 2006)

The teachers felt they were now clear about what they wanted students to learn and that they would know that students had learned it through the results of the formative assessment tasks they would create.

The group also determined that the last two questions, *What will we do if they don't learn it?* and *What will we do if they already know it?* would be addressed once they created three layers of learning. In other words, in addition to expectations for the application layer, they would create expectations for students who were currently in the essential knowledge layer of readiness, as well as expectations for students who could already perform the standard with proficiency. All students would be expected to eventually perform at least in the application layer, but some would need scaffolded instruction in order to get there.

They grouped assessment tasks into the following categories:

- Preassessment

- Informal assessment

- Growth assessment

- Final student product

Fourth Meeting: Determining the Language of the Standard

At the end of the fourth meeting, the teachers again looked at the standard in order to determine all of the terms and concepts that students would need to know in order to be successful with assessment. They created the grid shown in Table 6-4.

At the end of the fourth meeting, teachers of the Pleasantdale Elementary fifth-grade team also reviewed the progress and accomplishments of the previous five days. First, they had looked at data from fourth-grade assessments and portfolios to determine academic areas in which a large number of students were deficient. They had taken their district's goal for the school year into consideration as they narrowed down their list to the first area of concern for which they would create unit assessments. They had then analyzed this standard to make sure they understood the exact expectations for the learning. Finally, they had created a list of terms and concepts that both teachers and students would share as the common language during instruction and assessment. Their next job entailed creating the performance criteria and a rubric for assessment.

Fifth Meeting: Developing Performance Criteria and a Rubric

The teachers reviewed the components of performance criteria, recalling that they include the guidelines, rules, characteristics, or attributes that will be used to judge the quality of student performance. The performance criteria for this standard are shown on page 126.

Table 6-4. Words Associated With the Standard

Use reading strategies (for example, drawing conclusions, determining cause and effect, making inferences, sequencing) to comprehend text.

WORDS OF THE STANDARD (Words taken directly from the wording of the standard)	FREQUENT WORDS (Words students will see or hear often)	CONTENT WORDS (In this case, terms were chosen from the literature study, *The Sign of the Beaver*)	CHALLENGING WORDS (Words with more than one meaning)
PO 1. Use reading strategies to *draw conclusions* for reading comprehension.	drawing conclusions comprehension strategies evidence	Maine Native Americans chink in the log	conclusion
PO 2. Use reading strategies to determine *cause and effect* for reading comprehension.	cause and effect comprehension strategies	bear habitat action wilderness	relationship
PO 3. Use reading strategies to make *inferences* in reading comprehension.	making inferences comprehension strategies clues	culture beaver clan	
PO 4. Use reading strategies to *sequence* in reading comprehension.	sequence comprehension strategy signal words	events order signal words first	signal words

Following are the performance criteria for this standard:

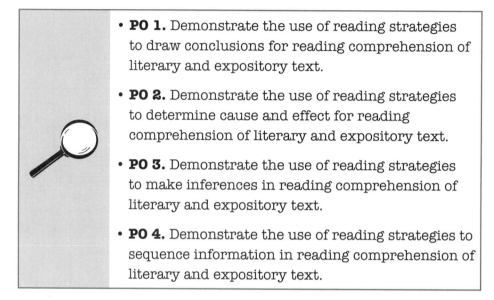

- **PO 1.** Demonstrate the use of reading strategies to draw conclusions for reading comprehension of literary and expository text.

- **PO 2.** Demonstrate the use of reading strategies to determine cause and effect for reading comprehension of literary and expository text.

- **PO 3.** Demonstrate the use of reading strategies to make inferences in reading comprehension of literary and expository text.

- **PO 4.** Demonstrate the use of reading strategies to sequence information in reading comprehension of literary and expository text.

Next, they asked themselves the following questions:

- Did we connect performance criteria to the standards?

- Did we choose a manageable number of performance criteria (3–5)?

- Did we create performance criteria that are measurable and teachable?

- Did we describe the performance criteria clearly?

- Did we verify that the book *The Sign of the Beaver* is an appropriate vehicle to target the content standards?

After the performance criteria were written, the teachers created the overall unit rubric, shown in Table 6-5. The rubric scoring tool listed both the performance criteria that would be used to judge student work and the degrees of quality for a piece of work. Since they had already created the performance criteria, only the performance tasks with the degrees of quality needed to be filled in. They created the following rubric with performance criteria attributes to describe the degrees of quality expected.

Table 6-5. Overall Unit Rubric

PERFORMANCE CRITERIA	EXEMPLARY 4	PROFICIENT 3	BASIC 2	NOVICE 1
Goal 1 Demonstrate the use of reading strategies to *draw conclusions* for reading comprehension of literary and expository text.	Independently draws conclusions with clear explanation and connections using evidence from the text and personal knowledge, ideas, or beliefs	With teacher prompts, draws conclusions with explanation using some evidence from the text and some personal knowledge or ideas	With guidance, draws some conclusions and shows a small amount of evidence from the text or personal knowledge	Attempts to draw conclusions without accuracy or demonstration of connections to evidence
Goal 2 Demonstrate the use of reading strategies to *determine cause and effect* for reading comprehension of literary and expository text.	Independently determines cause and effect with clear explanation and connections using evidence from the text and personal knowledge, ideas, or beliefs	With teacher prompts, determines cause and effect with explanation using some evidence from the text and some personal knowledge or ideas	With guidance, determines cause and effect and shows a small amount of evidence from the text or personal knowledge	Attempts to determine cause and effect without accuracy or demonstration of connections to evidence
Goal 3 Demonstrate the use of reading strategies to *make inferences* in reading comprehension of literary and expository text.	Independently makes predictions, interpretations, and inferences and clearly explains connections using evidence from the text and personal knowledge, ideas, or beliefs	With teacher prompts, makes some predictions or inferences with partial explanations using the text and personal knowledge or ideas	With guidance, makes some inferences and shows a small amount of evidence from the text or personal knowledge	Attempts to make predictions or inferences without accuracy or demonstration of connections to evidence
Goal 4 Demonstrate the use of reading strategies to *sequence information* in reading comprehension of literary and expository text.	Independently recognizes and uses sequencing as a reading strategy and clearly explains connections using evidence from the text and personal knowledge, ideas, or beliefs	With teacher prompts, recognizes and uses sequencing as a reading strategy with partial explanations using the text and personal knowledge or ideas	With guidance, recognizes and uses sequencing in reading and shows a small amount of evidence from the text or personal knowledge	Attempts to use sequencing as a reading strategy without accuracy or demonstration of connections to evidence

Before this meeting concluded, the teachers decided that they would research methods for assessing reading strategies and bring back some ideas for this reading standard. They decided to meet the following Wednesday to determine the formative assessment formats that would be most appropriate for this standard.

Sixth Meeting: Determining Focused Assessment Strategies and Formats

The teachers sat down to examine and question the current methods that they employed to help students use reading strategies for comprehension. Don Ryan urged the group to remain open to new possibilities for doing things better. The group decided to question themselves regarding their current proficiency in teaching and assessing reading strategies:

- What are we currently doing to teach students to use effective reading strategies?

- How are we currently assessing the use of effective reading strategies?

- Are we getting good results?

- How could we do it even better?

- What kinds of assessment formats would best assess this skill?

Because the teachers had determined that this standard was written in the application layer of learning, they wanted to make sure that they assigned appropriate assessment formats to fit that layer. They would also need to ensure that they created two additional layers of learning so that students who were not ready for the application layer could have customized lessons and activities to meet their level of readiness. And they also wanted to make certain, based on the preassessment and observation, that students who had already met or exceeded the application layer for this standard would be challenged with higher-level activities and instruction. They looked at the chart shown in Table 6-6 to see recommended assessment formats for each layer of learning.

Table 6-6. Strategies for Layers of Learning

INSTRUCTIONAL OR ASSESSMENT STRATEGIES	SPECIFIC ASSESSMENT LAYERS	
Essential Knowledge	Compare and contrast (rubric) Graphic organizers (rubric) Summarizing & note taking (rubric or O.C.L.) Journals (O.C.L. or rubric) Selected-response assessment (A.K.) 3-minute write (rubric or O.C.L.) Concept mapping (rubric or O.C.L.)	Semantic feature analysis (O.C.L.) Surveys (O.C.L.) Self-assessment (rubric) Computerized assessment (A.K.) Teacher-made assessment (A.K. or rubric) Textbook assessment (A.K.) Student-teacher conference (O.C.L.)
Application of Skills or Processes	Cooperative discussion (O.C.L.) Oral questioning (O.C.L.) Journals (O.C.L. or rubric) Problem-solving (rubric) Kinesthetic projects (rubric) Panels (O.C.L.) Concept mapping (rubric or O.C.L.) Project building (rubric) Graphic representations (rubric) Writing prompts (rubric or O.C.L.)	3-minute talk (rubric) Essay (rubric) Formal presentation (rubric) Surveys or interviews (O.C.L.) Self-assessment (rubric) Computerized assessment (A.K.) Teacher-made assessment (A.K. or rubric) Student-teacher conference (O.C.L.) Portfolio (rubric)
Complex Thinking	Research projects (rubric) Kinesthetic projects (rubric) Reflective discussion (O.C.L.) Double-entry journals (O.C.L. or rubric) Student critiquing (rubric) Evaluating (for example, author works—rubric) Essay (rubric) Experiments (rubric)	Formal presentation (rubric) Simulations (rubric) Writing prompts (rubric or O.C.L.) Oral questioning (O.C.L.) 3-minute talk (rubric) Self-assessment (rubric) Teacher-made assessment (A.K. or rubric) Student-teacher conference (O.C.L.) Portfolio (rubric)

O.C.L. = Observation Check List
A.K. = Answer Key

Next, they shared the strategies that they had researched and found to be highly effective for teaching reading comprehension strategies to students. They also shared a list of methods for assessing reading comprehension strategies and found that the instructional and assessment methods were often one and the same. For example, Jim Payne suggested that one of the teaching methods they could use was KWLT. This acronym stands for:

1. What do I *k*now?

2. What do I *w*ant to know?

3. What did I *l*earn?

4. What happened when I *t*ested it?

While this is an effective instructional strategy, it can also serve as a very comprehensive form of assessment in that it pre- and postassesses student knowledge. By the end of the meeting, they had created a lengthy list of ideas that, in most cases, could serve as instructional or assessment strategies.

Seventh Meeting: Preassessment, Informal Assessment, Growth Assessment, and Final Student Product

Now the teachers were feeling good about what they had accomplished so far. They met to finalize their chosen assessment formats and begin creating the assessments for the standard. Based on the strategies that they had shared at the previous meeting, they generated a grid to assign formative assessment strategies to the four categories that would be used throughout the unit. They then defined each phase of their formative assessment plan.

Preassessment. These include tools or activities used to measure current understanding of the goals or standard prior to the instruction. Examples include graphic organizers, learning journals, selected-response assessments, surveys, cooperative learning activities with teacher observation, as well as many other options.

Informal Assessment. These ongoing tools or activities will measure student progress and teacher effectiveness but will not be used for grades, as students are not expected to have mastered goals at this point. Students will receive explicit feedback during informal assessments whenever possible, to give them a focus for improvement.

Examples include teacher observation with checklists, graphic representations, teacher questioning, student self-assessments, and computer software programs.

Growth Assessment. These tools and activities will measure benchmark mastery of portions of the goals or standard. They may be translated into grades, as students will have received informal assessments with feedback prior to these assessments. Formats might include 3-minute talks, writing prompts, essays, multiple-choice quizzes, teacher-made tests, textbook review quizzes, or oral demonstration of knowledge with teachers.

Final Student Product. This will be a cumulative final picture of the students' understanding and mastery of the standard or goals. It will not be a test that is tacked on to the end of a lesson or unit but rather an accumulation, display, or presentation of student knowledge. This phase will generally include a student self-assessment of the learning.

The teachers chose the assessment designs shown in Table 6-7 that they felt would best meet the needs of their students for this particular standard.

Table 6-7. Assessment Design Grid

	PREASSESSMENT	INFORMAL ASSESSMENT	GROWTH ASSESSMENT	FINAL STUDENT PRODUCT
Teacher Observation With Checklist		Pre-made lists for various activities		
Graphic Organizer		Concept map	Students fill out strategy reminder list as they read.	
Writing Prompts	Students share current understanding of the four reading strategies		Students share current understanding of the four reading strategies	

(continued)

Table 6-7. Assessment Design Grid (continued)

	PREASSESSMENT	INFORMAL ASSESSMENT	GROWTH ASSESSMENT	FINAL STUDENT PRODUCT
Teacher Questioning		Modeling and questioning during oral reading		
3-Minute Talk				
Surveys or Interviews				
Kinesthetic Project				Students create a poster or other product to show what they know about strategies for reading comprehension.
Student Journals		Student explanation of how they've used one of the four reading strategies		
Student Self-Assessment				With rubric
Student Essay				
Oral Presentation				

(continued)

Table 6-7. Assessment Design Grid (continued)

	PREASSESSMENT	INFORMAL ASSESSMENT	GROWTH ASSESSMENT	FINAL STUDENT PRODUCT
Computerized Program		Reading comprehension program for practice and feedback		
Teacher-Made Assessment		Handout with passage; students read and answer questions to show understanding. Ungraded—provide explicit feedback		
Collaborative Sharing		Discussion in groups about using reading strategies		
Textbook Assessment			Students read a short story from reading book and complete reading strategy assessment in book.	
Student-Teacher Conference	Students listen to oral reading and ask questions.		Students listen to oral reading and ask questions.	Students listen to oral reading and ask questions.
Portfolios				
Selected-Response Assessment				

Next, the team wrote descriptions of what each assessment would entail and categorized the assessments according to the order in which they would be given.

Preassessment. The preassessment will consist of a writing prompt and an oral reading.

1. Writing Prompt. They will show the standard to students and then engage them in a brief discussion about effective reading comprehension strategies. The standards they will preview with students include the following:

- Drawing conclusions for reading comprehension
- Determining cause and effect for reading comprehension
- Making inferences
- Recognizing and following sequence for reading comprehension

They will give students a writing prompt like the one shown in Table 6-8 and ask them to divide their paper into four sections and describe how they might use the strategies before, during, or after reading. To determine student readiness for this skill, they will use a checklist like the one in Table 6-9. The indicators "more than ready," "ready," "somewhat ready," and "not ready" will be used as teachers read student papers.

Table 6-8. Student Writing Prompt

Drawing Conclusions	Determining Cause and Effect
What is it?	What is it?
How would I use it before, during, or after reading?	How would I use it before, during, or after reading?
Making Inferences	**Recognizing and Following Sequence**
What is it?	What is it?
How would I use it before, during, or after reading?	How would I use it before, during, or after reading?

Table 6-9. Student Readiness Checklist

DRAWING CONCLUSIONS	CAUSE AND EFFECT	MAKING INFERENCES	RECOGNIZING AND FOLLOWING SEQUENCE
4. More than ready	4. More than ready	4. More than ready	4. More than ready
3. Ready	3. Ready	3. Ready	3. Ready
2. Somewhat ready	2. Somewhat ready	2. Somewhat ready	2. Somewhat ready
1. Not ready	1. Not ready	1. Not ready	1. Not ready
Oral Reading With Questions		**Proficiency Level**	
Which strategies did student attempt?		What is the current readiness level?	
Assessment 1:		Assessment 1:	
Assessment 2:		Assessment 2:	
Assessment 3:		Assessment 3:	

2. Oral Reading With Questions. During morning work, teachers will call back small groups of students to read passages from *The Sign of the Beaver.* They will ask students to demonstrate one or more of the four reading strategies as they read. For instance, students might list the sequence of events and note the signal words that were used to show the sequence. Teachers will use the same checklist to add this new data about students' readiness.

Informal Assessment. The informal assessment will consist of a variety of formats.

1. Teacher Observations. Informal assessment will occur throughout the teaching and learning activities. It is not feasible for teachers to use a checklist in the middle of instruction, but when students work on tasks, they can walk around to record their observations on the checklist. The checklist headings are as follows:

- Incomplete or inaccurate
- Complete and somewhat accurate
- Complete and accurate

2. Concept Map. During the first formal lesson on these four reading strategies, teachers will ask students to fill out a concept map like the one in Figure 6-1, listing the steps involved in each strategy. They will use the same checklist to record the level of current student understanding.

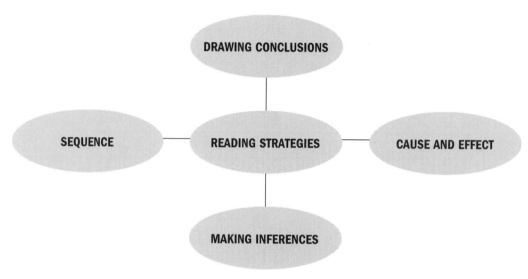

Figure 6-1. Concept Map

3. Modeling and Questioning. Throughout the teaching and learning of these reading strategies, the Pleasantdale teachers plan to model the process of using reading for comprehension strategies with phrases like, "Hmmm, I'm going to draw the conclusion that Matt is going to get stung by the bees because he has no experience with gathering honey." Then they will begin asking students questions so they can practice these new skills. This assessment doesn't necessarily require a checklist, but the teachers will make mental notes about how well students are able to begin using these strategies after modeling and prompting.

4. Student Explanation in Journals. After students have had opportunities to use these strategies with teacher modeling and student prompting, the teachers will provide opportunities for them to practice in collaborative groups of four. They will give one card to each member of the team and then direct members to read a passage orally. Each card will have one of four strategies written on it: One person will try to draw conclusions about the passage, another will determine cause and effect, a third will attempt to make inferences, and the fourth will find sequences in the passage.

Following this activity, members will go back to their seats to create journal entries. They will then share which card they had been given and how successful they were in using the reading strategy. Teachers will write back to students in the journals to share specific feedback and encouragement for using the new strategies.

5. *Computerized Program.* Each teacher will have a reading comprehension practice program that ties into the novel *The Sign of the Beaver.* This will give students additional practice in using the four reading strategies. They will print a score for students when they complete a practice session; this will give them one more opportunity to formulate a picture of students' current ability to use these strategies.

6. *Handout With Passage.* The Pleasantdale teachers will give students a teacher-made assessment that will not be used for a grade but will show both them and their students the current level of understanding. They will give students explicit feedback on their strategy use.

7. *Collaborative Sharing.* Collaborative sharing will occur when students are involved in the card activity. Groups will have opportunities to share journal entries with each other to learn more about their respective strategies.

Growth Assessment. The growth assessment will also consist of a variety of formats.

1. *Strategy Reminder List.* The teachers will give students a strategy reminder list, shown in Table 6-10, to use during the reading of a passage as they practice the skills of drawing conclusions, cause and effect, making inferences, and sequencing. They will score this with a rubric and use it as part of the accumulated scores that will be translated into grades.

Table 6-10. Strategy Reminder List

1. Based on evidence or facts, what conclusions can you draw as you are reading? Conclusion 1: Conclusion 2: Conclusion 3:	2. Causes → →	→ → Effects
3. From hints, clues, evidence, or facts in the passage, ask and answer questions that start with who, what, when, how, or why.	4. Sequencing: As you read the passage, make a sequential list of the story events using only the main or important ideas of the story.	

2. *Writing Prompt.* Teachers will provide a prompt for all four strategies and ask students to share their current understanding and example for each strategy. This will be scored with a rubric.

3. Textbook Assessment. Teachers will ask students to read a nonfiction selection that requires them to use the four reading strategies and answer questions at the end of the selection. The teachers may want to score these and compile them later with other growth-assessment scores.

4. Oral Reading With Questions. This time, when students read a passage orally and the teachers prompt them to share the reading strategies that they are using, the teachers will score the checklist and compile it with the other growth assessment scores, as students will by then have had specific feedback and practice in this skill. The teachers could use the same checklist that was used in the preassessment, Table 6-9 on page 135.

Final Student Project: Poster Project for Reading Strategies. The teachers will then ask students to create a poster for each of the reading strategies that they practiced. The created posters will demonstrate their own definitions and example(s) of the strategy. Table 6-11 shows the performance criteria for the poster project.

Table 6-11. Poster Project Performance Rubric

PERFORMANCE CRITERIA	4 AWESOME & INSIGHTFUL	3 PLEASING & PROFICIENT	2 ON YOUR WAY	1 NEWBIE OR NOVICE
Demonstrate accurate text example and illustration of *drawing conclusions* from reading selection.	Examples represent an accurate and clear understanding of drawing conclusions in reading.	Examples represent a fair and mostly clear understanding of drawing conclusions in reading.	Examples represent a partial and somewhat clear understanding of drawing conclusions in reading.	Examples represent little or no understanding of drawing conclusions in reading.
Demonstrate accurate text example and illustration of *cause and effect* from reading selection.	Examples represent an accurate and clear understanding of cause and effect in reading.	Examples represent a fair and mostly clear understanding of cause and effect in reading.	Examples represent a partial and somewhat clear understanding of cause and effect in reading.	Examples represent little or no understanding of cause and effect in reading.
Demonstrate accurate text example and illustration of *making inferences* from reading selection.	Examples represent an accurate and clear understanding of making inferences in reading.	Examples represent a fair and mostly clear understanding of making inferences in reading.	Examples represent a partial and somewhat clear understanding of making inferences in reading.	Examples represent little or no understanding of making inferences in reading.
Demonstrate accurate text example and illustration of *sequence* from reading selection.	Examples represent an accurate and clear understanding of sequence in reading.	Examples represent a fair and mostly clear understanding of sequence in reading.	Examples represent a partial and somewhat clear understanding of sequence in reading.	Examples represent little or no understanding of sequence in reading.

1. Student Self-Assessment. The Pleasantdale teachers will encourage students to self-reflect and self-assess throughout the learning process. The students will use several templates for "during learning" assessments, but will use the one shown in Table 6-12, Strategies and Thinking Skills, for the final assessment, as it will give them the opportunity to reflect on their learning. Students will use this reflection rubric for each of the posters that they create.

Table 6-12. Strategies and Thinking Skills

Strategy Used:_____

1	2	3	4
I could not figure out how to start or didn't know what strategy to use.	I got started but don't know how to finish, or I need more help.	I think I've got it figured out but don't have total confidence yet.	I understand the strategy and can apply it to my reading. I could show others how to use this strategy.
Explanation:	Explanation:	Explanation:	Explanation:

2. Oral Reading With Questions. The teachers will call back small groups of students to read passages for the third time. They will ask students to demonstrate each reading strategy as they read, and prompt or ask questions if students continue to need help. They will also use the same rubric checklist that was used in the growth assessment, Table 6-10 on page 137, to show progress in employing these strategies.

Eighth Meeting: Customizing the Expectations for the Standard

At this point, the teachers needed to review the suggested assessment formats to determine how they would customize the learning for students who will be in the essential knowledge, application, and complex-thinking layers of learning. This would be determined by their initial preassessment as well as their observation and knowledge of student abilities.

The teachers created a list of expectations for their learners, with the awareness that it needed to be fluid and flexible. Some learners who they initially thought were in the essential knowledge layer may demonstrate that they are ready to take on the expectations of the application layer. Similarly, some students who were thought to be ready for the complex-thinking layer might demonstrate that they are not quite ready for the extra challenge. The teachers created the performance criteria in Table 6-13 for each of the layers of learning.

Table 6-13. Performance Criteria for Layered Learning

ESSENTIAL KNOWLEDGE LAYER	APPLICATION LAYER	COMPLEX-THINKING LAYER
Students will demonstrate independent and proficient use of two of the reading strategies with proficiency.	Student will demonstrate independent and proficient use of all four reading strategies.	Students will demonstrate independent use of all four reading strategies as well as the strategy of SQ3R.

Next, they modified the initial rubric that would be used after the final-product phase of the learning, so that they had three different rubrics, one for each of the three layers of learning, as shown in Tables 6-14 to 6-16 on pages 141–43. Again, all students were expected to eventually meet at least the application layer, which is the layer that the standard calls for.

Table 6-14. Essential Knowledge Layer Rubric

PERFORMANCE CRITERIA	EXEMPLARY 4	PROFICIENT 3	BASIC 2	NOVICE 1
Goal 1: Demonstrate the use of reading strategies to *draw conclusions* for reading comprehension of literary and expository text.	Independently draws conclusions with clear explanation and connections using evidence from the text and personal knowledge, ideas, or beliefs	With teacher prompts, draws conclusions with explanation using some evidence from the text and some personal knowledge or ideas	With guidance, draws some conclusions and shows a small amount of evidence from the text or personal knowledge	Attempts to draw conclusions without accuracy or demonstration of connections to evidence
Goal 2: Demonstrate the use of reading strategies to *determine cause and effect* for reading comprehension of literary and expository text.	Independently determines cause and effect with clear explanation and connections using evidence from the text and personal knowledge, ideas, or beliefs	With teacher prompts, determines cause and effect with explanation using some evidence from the text and some personal knowledge or ideas	With guidance, determines cause and effect and shows a small amount of evidence from the text or personal knowledge	Attempts to determine cause and effect without accuracy or demonstration of connections to evidence
Goal 3: Demonstrate the use of reading strategies to *make inferences* in reading comprehension of literary and expository text.	This goal will be addressed after student is proficient in the first two strategies.			
Goal 4: Demonstrate the use of reading strategies to *sequence* information in reading comprehension of literary and expository text.	This goal will be addressed after student is proficient in the first two strategies.			

Table 6-15. Application Layer Rubric

PERFORMANCE CRITERIA	EXEMPLARY 4	PROFICIENT 3	BASIC 2	NOVICE 1
Goal 1: Demonstrate the use of reading strategies to *draw conclusions* for reading comprehension of literary and expository text.	Independently draws conclusions with clear explanation and connections using evidence from the text and personal knowledge, ideas, or beliefs	With teacher prompts, draws conclusions with explanation using some evidence from the text and some personal knowledge or ideas	With guidance, draws some conclusions and shows a small amount of evidence from the text or personal knowledge	Attempts to draw conclusions without accuracy or demonstration of connections to evidence
Goal 2: Demonstrate the use of reading strategies to *determine cause and effect* for reading comprehension of literary and expository text.	Independently determines cause and effect with clear explanation and connections using evidence from the text and personal knowledge, ideas, or beliefs	With teacher prompts, determines cause and effect with explanation using some evidence from the text and some personal knowledge or ideas	With guidance, determines cause and effect and shows a small amount of evidence from the text or personal knowledge	Attempts to determine cause and effect without accuracy or demonstration of connections to evidence
Goal 3: Demonstrate the use of reading strategies to *make inferences* in reading comprehension of literary and expository text.	Independently makes predictions, interpretations, and inferences and clearly explains connections using evidence from the text and personal knowledge, ideas, or beliefs	With teacher prompts, makes some predictions, or inferences with partial explanations using the text and personal knowledge or ideas	With guidance, makes some inferences and shows a small amount of evidence from the text or personal knowledge	Attempts to make predictions or inferences without accuracy or demonstration of connections to evidence
Goal 4: Demonstrate the use of reading strategies to *sequence* information in reading comprehension of literary and expository text.	Independently recognizes and uses sequencing as a reading strategy and clearly explains connections using evidence from the text and personal knowledge, ideas, or beliefs	With teacher prompts, recognizes and uses sequencing as a reading strategy with partial explanations using the text and personal knowledge or ideas	With guidance, recognizes and uses sequencing in reading and shows a small amount of evidence from the text or personal knowledge	Attempts to use sequencing as a reading strategy without accuracy or demonstration of connections to evidence

Table 6-16. Complex-Thinking Layer Rubric

PERFORMANCE CRITERIA	EXEMPLARY 4	PROFICIENT 3	BASIC 2	NOVICE 1
Goal 1: Demonstrate the use of reading strategies to *draw conclusions* for reading comprehension of literary and expository text.	Independently draws conclusions with clear explanation and connections using evidence from the text and personal knowledge, ideas, or beliefs	With teacher prompts, draws conclusions with explanation using some evidence from the text and some personal knowledge or ideas	With guidance, draws some conclusions and shows a small amount of evidence from the text or personal knowledge	Attempts to draw conclusions without accuracy or demonstration of connections to evidence
Goal 2: Demonstrate the use of reading strategies to *determine cause and effect* for reading comprehension of literary and expository text.	Independently determines cause and effect with clear explanation and connections using evidence from the text and personal knowledge, ideas, or beliefs	With teacher prompts, determines cause and effect with explanation using some evidence from the text and some personal knowledge or ideas	With guidance, determines cause and effect and shows a small amount of evidence from the text or personal knowledge	Attempts to determine cause and effect without accuracy or demonstration of connections to evidence
Goal 3: Demonstrate the use of reading strategies to *make inferences* in reading comprehension of literary and expository text.	Independently makes predictions, interpretations, and inferences and clearly explains connections using evidence from the text and personal knowledge, ideas, or beliefs	With teacher prompts, makes some predictions, or inferences with partial explanations using the text and personal knowledge or ideas	With guidance, makes some inferences and shows a small amount of evidence from the text or personal knowledge	Attempts to make predictions or inferences without accuracy or demonstration of connections to evidence
Goal 4: Demonstrate the use of reading strategies to *sequence information* in reading comprehension of literary and expository text.	Independently recognizes and uses sequencing as a reading strategy and clearly explains connections using evidence from the text and personal knowledge, ideas, or beliefs	With teacher prompts, recognizes and uses sequencing as a reading strategy with partial explanations using the text and personal knowledge or ideas	With guidance, recognizes and uses sequencing in reading and shows a small amount of evidence from the text or personal knowledge	Attempts to use sequencing as a reading strategy without accuracy or demonstration of connections to evidence
Goal 5: Demonstrate the use of reading SQ3R reading strategy for comprehension of literary and expository text.	Independently uses SQ3R as a reading strategy and clearly explains connections using evidence from the text and personal knowledge, ideas, or beliefs	With teacher prompts, uses SQ3R as a reading strategy with partial connection explanations using the text and personal knowledge or ideas	With guidance, uses SQ3R in reading and shows a small amount of evidence from the text or personal knowledge	Attempts to use SQ3R as a reading strategy without accuracy or demonstration of connections to evidence

Ninth Meeting: Evaluating Assessment Prior to Implementation

The teachers will, of course, meet throughout the learning process and assess the effectiveness of their chosen assessments. However, prior to the actual teaching and assessing of this unit, they wanted to review their choices to ensure that they had created a quality plan for this standard. The evaluation form in Table 6-17 is an effective tool for reviewing an assessment plan prior to putting it in action. They will fill out the last section after the completion of the unit.

Table 6-17. Assessment Evaluation

Content/Standard			
1. Formats are conducive to testing this particular content.	Yes	No	Somewhat
2. There are enough assessment tasks to accumulate a comprehensive picture of student proficiency with this skill.	Yes	No	Somewhat
3. The assessment tasks reflect all of the expectations of the standard.	Yes	No	Somewhat
4. Performance criteria and performance tasks are congruent.	Yes	No	Somewhat
5. Rubrics created reflect the performance criteria.	Yes	No	Somewhat
6. Learning targets are clearly stated in performance criteria, rubric, and tasks.	Yes	No	Somewhat
Meeting Learner Needs			
1. Assessment tasks take various learning styles into consideration.	Yes	No	Somewhat
2. Rubric has been created so that varying ability levels and diverse learners will have needs met.	Yes	No	Somewhat
3. Assessment tasks and tools will enable students to be involved in the assessment process.	Yes	No	Somewhat
4. Includes content, examples, tasks, and context that are equally familiar and appropriate for students of all backgrounds and cultures.	Yes	No	Somewhat
Reflecting on Results			
1. Assessment provides relevant information about students' level of understanding.	Yes	No	Somewhat
2. Assessment results of teachers in varying classrooms show similar numbers of students who are proficient and not proficient.	Yes	No	Somewhat
3. Results from all classrooms who participated show that assessment task results are reliable.	Yes	No	Somewhat
4. Rubric consistencies of all classrooms who participated demonstrate valid assessment tasks.	Yes	No	Somewhat

The Pleasantdale team is now ready to launch its first attempt at using common assessment. They have set a timeframe of 3 weeks to complete this unit on reading comprehension strategies and will continue to meet in their group once a week to check in with each other and share ideas. At the end of the 3 weeks, they will enter a new phase—that of assessing their results.

Thinking About Your Thinking

The fifth-grade teachers of Pleasantdale Elementary know that they don't have all the answers to creating common assessment. They recognize that in order for their assessment plan to be effective, it must be viewed as an ever-evolving, changing, and growing design. If you had been involved in the creation of this unit plan, what suggestions or thoughts would you have shared regarding preassessment, informal assessment, growth assessment, and final student producs? How might you have customized the assessment tasks differently?

Tools and Templates

The resources in this section can also be found online at teachinginfocus.com.

Tool 22: Performance Criteria

Performance Criteria:

_____

_____

Overall Standard or Goal:

_____

_____

Goal 1:
Goal 2:
Goal 3:
Goal 4:

After completing your performance criteria, check yourselves with these questions:

Did I connect performance criteria to the standards?

Did I choose a manageable number of performance criteria (3–5)?

Did I create performance criteria that are measurable and teachable?

Did I describe the performance criteria clearly?

Tool 23: Strategies for Layers of Learning

Assessment Layers: Instructional Strategies

INSTRUCTIONAL OR ASSESSMENT STRATEGIES	SPECIFIC ASSESSMENT LAYERS	
Essential Knowledge	Compare and contrast (rubric)	Semantic feature analysis (O.C.L.)
	Graphic organizers (rubric)	Surveys (O.C.L.)
	Summarizing & note taking (rubric or O.C.L.)	Self-assessment (rubric)
	Journals (O.C.L. or rubric)	Computerized assessment (A.K.)
	Selected-response assessment (A.K.)	Teacher-made assessment (A.K. or rubric)
	3-minute write (rubric or O.C.L.)	Textbook assessment (A.K.)
	Concept mapping (rubric or O.C.L.)	Student-teacher conference (O.C.L.)
Application of Skills or Processes	Cooperative discussion (O.C.L.)	3-minute talk (rubric)
	Oral questioning (O.C.L.)	Essay (rubric)
	Journals (O.C.L. or rubric)	Formal presentation (rubric)
	Problem-solving (rubric)	Surveys or interviews (O.C.L.)
	Kinesthetic projects (rubric)	Self-assessment (rubric)
	Panels (O.C.L.)	Computerized assessment (A.K.)
	Concept mapping (rubric or O.C.L.)	Teacher-made assessment (A.K. or rubric)
	Project building (rubric)	Student-teacher conference (O.C.L.)
	Graphic representations (rubric)	Portfolio (rubric)
	Writing prompts (rubric or O.C.L.)	
Complex Thinking	Research projects (rubric)	Formal presentation (rubric)
	Kinesthetic projects (rubric)	Simulations (rubric)
	Reflective discussion (O.C.L.)	Writing prompts (rubric or O.C.L.)
	Double-entry journals (O.C.L. or rubric)	Oral questioning (O.C.L.)
	Student critiquing (rubric)	3-minute talk (rubric)
	Evaluating (for example, author works—rubric)	Self-assessment (rubric)
		Teacher-made assessment (A.K. or rubric)
	Essay (rubric)	Student-teacher conference (O.C.L.)
	Experiments (rubric)	Portfolio (rubric)

O.C.L. = Observation Check List
A.K. = Answer Key

Tool 24: Assessment Design Grid

Remember that the preassessment and all informal assessments measure current student knowledge or understanding. Scores that will be accumulated and eventually translated into grades should come from the growth assessments and final student products.

	PREASSESSMENT	INFORMAL ASSESSMENT	GROWTH ASSESSMENT	FINAL STUDENT PRODUCT
Teacher Observation With Checklist				
Graphic Organizer				
Writing Prompts				
Teacher Questioning				
3-Minute Talk				
Surveys or Interviews				
Kinesthetic Project				
Student Journals				

(continued)

Tool 24: Assessment Design Grid (continued)

	PREASSESSMENT	INFORMAL ASSESSMENT	GROWTH ASSESSMENT	FINAL STUDENT PRODUCT
Student Self-Assessment				
Student Essay				
Oral Presentation				
Computerized Program				
Teacher-Made Assessment				
Collaborative Sharing				
Textbook Assessment				
Student-Teacher Conference				
Portfolios				
Selected-Response Assessment				

Tool 25: Oral Reading With Teacher Questions or Prompts

How Ready Are They?

Directions: Students read a passage orally and are prompted to share the reading strategies that they are using. The same checklist used in the preassessment, informal assessment, and growth assessment may be used again as part of the final student product.

Reading Strategy:	Reading Strategy:	Reading Strategy:	Reading Strategy:
_____	_____	_____	_____
More Than Ready	More Than Ready	More Than Ready	More Than Ready
Ready	Ready	Ready	Ready
Somewhat Ready	Somewhat Ready	Somewhat Ready	Somewhat Ready
Not Ready	Not Ready	Not Ready	Not Ready
Assessment 1:	Assessment 1:	Assessment 1:	Assessment 1:
Assessment 2:	Assessment 2:	Assessment 2:	Assessment 2:
Assessment 3:	Assessment 3:	Assessment 3:	Assessment 3:

Tool 26: Checklist for Teacher Observation

During Student Independent Practice

Skill being observed:

STUDENT NAMES	INCOMPLETE OR INACCURATE	COMPLETE AND SOMEWHAT ACCURATE	COMPLETE AND ACCURATE

(continued)

Tool 26: Checklist for Teacher Observation (continued)

STUDENT NAMES	INCOMPLETE OR INACCURATE	COMPLETE AND SOMEWHAT ACCURATE	COMPLETE AND ACCURATE

Tool 27: Reading Reminder List

Student Directions: Read a passage as you practice the skills of drawing conclusions, identifying cause and effect, making inferences, and sequencing.

1. Based on evidence or facts, what conclusions can you draw as you are reading? Conclusion 1: Conclusion 2: Conclusion 3:	2. Causes → →	→ → Effects
3. From hints, clues, evidence, or facts in the passage, ask and answer questions that start with who, what, when, how, or why.	4. Sequencing: As you read the passage, make a sequential list of the story events using only the main or important ideas of the story.	

Tool 28: Performance Criteria for Layered Learning

After determining which layer of learning the content standard is asking for, customize the learning into three layers—for students in the essential knowledge, application, and complex-thinking layers of learning. This should be determined on the basis of the initial preassessment as well as your observation and knowledge of student abilities.

This list needs to be fluid and flexible. Some learners who are initially thought to be in the essential knowledge layer may demonstrate that they are ready to take on the expectations of the application layer. Some students who had complex-thinking expectations may demonstrate that they are not ready for the extra challenge.

ESSENTIAL KNOWLEDGE LAYER	APPLICATION LAYER	COMPLEX-THINKING LAYER

Next, modify the initial rubric, so that you have three different rubrics, one for each of the three layers of learning. Again, all students would ultimately be expected to meet the expectations of the standard.

Tool 29: Poster Project for Reading Strategies

Students were asked to create a poster for each of the reading strategies that they had practiced. The posters demonstrated their own definition and example(s) of the strategy. Teachers would therefore use this rubric two times if students were in the essential knowledge layer, four times if students were in the application layer, and five times if students were in the complex-thinking layer of learning.

PERFORMANCE CRITERIA	4 AWESOME & INSIGHTFUL	3 PLEASING & PROFICIENT	2 ON YOUR WAY	1 NEWBIE OR NOVICE
Demonstrate accurate text example and illustration of *drawing conclusions* from reading selection.	Examples represent an accurate and clear understanding of drawing conclusions in reading.	Examples represent a fair and mostly clear understanding of drawing conclusions in reading.	Examples represent a partial and somewhat clear understanding of drawing conclusions in reading.	Examples represent little or no understanding of drawing conclusions in reading.
Demonstrate accurate text example and illustration of *cause and effect* from reading selection.	Examples represent an accurate and clear understanding of cause and effect in reading.	Examples represent a fair and mostly clear understanding of cause and effect in reading.	Examples represent a partial and somewhat clear understanding of cause and effect in reading.	Examples represent little or no understanding of cause and effect in reading.
Demonstrate accurate text example and illustration of *making inferences* from reading selection.	Examples represent an accurate and clear understanding of making inferences in reading.	Examples represent a fair and mostly clear understanding of making inferences in reading.	Examples represent a partial and somewhat clear understanding of making inferences in reading.	Examples represent little or no understanding of making inferences in reading.
Demonstrate accurate text example and illustration of *sequence* from reading selection.	Examples represent an accurate and clear understanding of sequence in reading.	Examples represent a fair and mostly clear understanding of sequence in reading.	Examples represent a partial and somewhat clear understanding of sequence in reading.	Examples represent little or no understanding of sequence in reading.

Tool 30: Assessment Evaluation

Content/Standard			
1. Formats are conducive to testing this particular content.	Yes	No	Somewhat
2. There are enough assessment tasks to accumulate a comprehensive picture of student proficiency with this skill.	Yes	No	Somewhat
3. The assessment tasks reflect all of the expectations of the standard.	Yes	No	Somewhat
4. Performance criteria and performance tasks are congruent.	Yes	No	Somewhat
5. Rubrics created reflect the performance criteria.	Yes	No	Somewhat
6. Learning targets are clearly stated in performance criteria, rubric, and tasks.	Yes	No	Somewhat
Meeting Learner Needs			
1. Assessment tasks take various learning styles into consideration.	Yes	No	Somewhat
2. Rubric has been created so that varying ability levels and diverse learners will have needs met.	Yes	No	Somewhat
3. Assessment tasks and tools will enable students to be involved in the assessment process.	Yes	No	Somewhat
4. Includes content, examples, tasks, and context that are equally familiar and appropriate for students of all backgrounds and cultures.	Yes	No	Somewhat
Reflecting on Results			
1. Assessment provides relevant information about students' level of understanding.	Yes	No	Somewhat
2. Assessment results of teachers in varying classrooms show similar numbers of students who are proficient and not proficient.	Yes	No	Somewhat
3. Results from all classrooms who participated show that assessment task results are reliable.	Yes	No	Somewhat
4. Rubric consistencies of all classrooms who participated demonstrate valid assessment tasks.	Yes	No	Somewhat

Launching the Unit and Reflecting on the Results

Making a commitment to link standards also means making a commitment to report progress in relation to those standards.

—Judy F. Carr and Douglas E. Harris

In this chapter . . .

- Thinking About Assessment
- Launching the Unit
- Mr. Payne's Class
- Looking at Test Results
- Converting Scores Into Grades
- Final Thoughts
- Tools and Templates

Thinking About Assessment

Anytime you launch a new unit, lesson plan, assessment, or teaching method, you have made a judgment based on your knowledge or research that it is a sound practice and will achieve good results. Sometimes your strategies aren't as effective as you hope they will be, but you should always give yourself credit for exploring new territory. And instead of saying, "Oh well, that one bombed," using a focused assessment approach enables you to analyze how effective the plan was, what pieces worked, what pieces didn't, and what could have been done differently—and to make changes based on results.

Our Pleasantdale Elementary team is now ready to launch its first unit comprised of common assessments. From this experience, they will learn to take more risks, analyze their results, and go on to new challenges.

Launching the Unit

All the teachers agreed to use the focused instruction model so that their teaching practices would be similar during the next 3 weeks. The focused instruction model encompasses research-based features of the existing models of direct instruction, indirect instruction, and differentiated instruction. To follow a step-by-step guide, they used *Focused Instruction: An Innovative Teaching Model for All Learners* and the tools it contains to support diverse learners.

Mr. Payne's Class

Goals and Purpose

Mr. Payne told his students exactly what they were expected to learn and why they should learn it:

> In today's lesson, you will be learning about the importance of using specific reading strategies to help you with comprehension. Throughout our 3-week unit, we'll be reading a book called *The Sign of the Beaver,* a story about a boy who must learn to survive among early Native Americans in the year 1768. While we read this book, we will also be exploring four of the best strategies for reading comprehension: drawing conclusions, cause and effect, making inferences, and using sequences in reading.

He points to the whiteboard on which the standard is listed and asks a student to read it. He spends a few minutes letting students discuss what the standard is asking them to know or do.

> Use reading strategies (for example, drawing conclusions, determining cause and effect, making inferences, sequencing) to comprehend text.

Brain Activators

Research shows that students learn and retain information better when they can associate it with something that they already know. Mr. Payne asks students to do the following exercise: "Divide your paper into four sections. List the four teaching strategies, and share what you already know about each one of them. How can they help you with reading comprehension?"

Learning the Language of the Standard

In order to be more successful in learning the new information, students need to know the terms and concept words that will be used during the lesson. They therefore use a graphic organizer while Mr. Payne teaches them the language of the standard. The Pleasantdale teachers had predetermined the words of the standard they wanted to preteach, along with words that would be spoken or read frequently, additional content words related to the standard, and challenging words. As a result, Mr. Payne feels very clear about the concepts and terms he must teach in order for students to be successful with the learning.

Sequential and Active Instruction

As he teaches, he knows that students need to be *doing*—taking notes, discussing the material, role playing, drawing diagrams, and getting involved in activities that get them out of their seats. He must also take into account the readiness levels and needs of individual students. In customizing the lessons to meet the needs of all students, he divides learning expectations into 3 layers:

1. Essential knowledge layer

2. Application layer

3. Complex-thinking layer

Checking for Understanding

This step is part of the formative assessment process, as the teacher is continuously checking for the level of students' understanding. During the planning of common assessments, the Pleasantdale Elementary fifth-grade team chose assessment designs for a pretest, and for informal assessment, growth assessment, and final student product. Mr. Payne therefore feels confident that he has multiple avenues for checking the understanding and knowledge levels of his students.

Student Practice With Scaffolding

After instruction, students need an opportunity to practice what has been taught. Practice takes place through partner work, solving problems, journaling, and a variety of other means. The following are the scaffolded levels of student practice:

- Controlled practice—Following teacher modeling, students receive clear expectations for a task. Mr. Payne and his students work through the task together, using discussion and feedback.

- Coached practice—Following explicit instructions for task expectations, students take more responsibility for the learning but are monitored and guided by the teacher. This phase involves cues, prompts, questions, and feedback from Mr. Payne.

- Independent practice—After receiving clear expectations for the learning, students work independently on the learning task. The teacher continues to provide cues, prompts, or feedback as needed, but transfers the responsibility for learning to the students.

Being conscious of the layers of learning that the group created (see Table 6-14 on page 141), Mr. Payne asks the students in the complex-thinking layer to practice five strategies, he asks students currently in the application layer to practice four strategies, and asks students in the essential knowledge layer to concentrate on two reading strategies.

Teacher Feedback

Feedback occurs each day in each lesson and with each activity in which students are engaged. Mr. Payne continuously assesses and provides explicit information to students about what they are doing well and what they could be doing better, along with suggestions for improvement. Feedback can happen in small conference groups that include the teacher and several students, or it can be given through written suggestions or one-on-one discussions as students continue to work on the assignment. This is another form of assessment, as well as a way to involve students in the learning process.

Final Student Product

Mr. Payne's final student products for the reading strategies unit are 1) a poster project, 2) student self-assessment, and 3) oral reading with the teacher to demonstrate the use of reading strategies. Prior to the final product, students will be involved in multiple demonstrations of learning throughout the 3 weeks, as they learn to use reading strategies.

Student Reflections

Students need opportunities to express what they have learned or to share their feelings about the newly learned concepts through journaling, partner discussions, group interaction, whole class dialogue, and similar activities.

Looking at Test Results

The teachers had previously discussed the need to strictly adhere to the performance criteria that they had written prior to creating the rubric assessments. Students had been given each rubric at the beginning of the lesson to which the rubric pertained, so that they would have a clear focus from the beginning regarding the expectations for the learning.

Teachers scored each assessment independently based on the rubric. They made note of any inconsistencies that stood out, as well as items or complete assessments that had surprising results.

After the first 3 weeks of school, the group got back together to analyze their results. They consciously stayed focused on student performance data from the growth and final product assessments. They knew that all previous steps would be useless if the team forgot its focus on tangible improvements. The teachers looked at test scores, rubric results, sample papers, and any other evidence that they deemed relevant to their mission. Although individual teachers had gained valuable information from the preassessment and various informal assessments, only the growth and final student product results were reviewed in this session.

They asked the following questions:

- What does our classroom data tell us about student performance in using reading strategies?

- Which assessments show inconsistencies or varying results?

- What criteria will we use to measure our success?

- Was this common assessment effort successful for student learning? What is our evidence of that?

- What could we have done differently to improve our results?

Each teacher on the team brought a cumulative record for easier data analysis and comparisons of the results. Mr. Payne's records are shown in Tables 7-1 and 7-2, on pages 163–164.

The teachers analyzed their results by individual classrooms and common incorrect responses made by students throughout all classrooms. Here is what they wanted to know:

By individual student, which of the following was the cause of the deficiency?

- Higher order questions

- Certain content areas

- Lack of reading/writing proficiency

- Lack of cultural relevance

- Emotional/social student situation

In looking at common incorrect responses by individual classroom, they asked the following:

- Were students' incorrect responses consistent or varied?

- Was the topic or content taught at a great enough depth in deficient areas?

In looking at common incorrect responses among all classrooms that administered these common assessments, the teachers asked these questions:

- Were students' incorrect responses consistent or varied?

- Were the assessment questions and directions worded clearly?

This would help them to know which test items should be modified and changed.

Table 7-1. Cumulative Scoring Record for Growth Assessmen

GROWTH ASSESSMENT	SCORING TOOL	TOTALS BY CLASSROOM			

Strategy Reminder List
Students were given a strategy reminder list to use during the reading of a passage as they practiced the skills of drawing conclusions, cause and effect, making inferences, and sequencing. This was scored with a rubric and used as part of the cumulative score that will be translated into grades.
	Rubric
	
	Total taking test: 29
	
	Total taking test: 29
	
	Total taking test: 26
	
	Total taking test: 26
		4 3 2 1
		Drawing Conclusions
		    (10) (5) (10) (4)
		Cause and Effect
		    (9) (8) (9) (3)
		Inferences
		    (9) (7) (6) (4)
		Sequence
		    (8) (6) (8) (4)			

Writing Prompt
Teachers provided a prompt for all four strategies (two prompts for the essential knowledge layer and five for the complex-thinking layer) and asked students to share their current understanding and an example for each strategy. This was scored with a rubric.
	Rubric
	
	Total taking test: 29
	
	Total taking test: 29
	
	Total taking test: 26
	
	Total taking test: 26
		4 3 2 1
		Drawing Conclusions
		    (8) (5) (11) (5)
		Cause and Effect
		    (7) (5) (12) (5)
		Inferences
		    (7) (8) (8) (3)
		Sequence
		    (8) (9) (7) (2)			

Textbook Assessment Students were asked to read a nonfiction selection from the text that required them to use the four reading strategies (with two selections for the essential knowledge layer and five for the complex-thinking layer) and answer questions at the end of the selection. This was scored and compiled with other growth assessment scores.	**Answer Key** 90–100 = A 80–89 = B 70–79 = C 60–69 = D	Total students taking test: 29 A–7 students B–10 students C–6 students D–5 students F–1 student			

Oral Reading With Questions
Students read a passage orally and were prompted to share the reading strategies that they were using. The checklist was scored and compiled with the other growth assessment scores, as students received specific feedback and practice in this skill. The same checklist that was used in the preassessment was used again in order to observe student growth.
	Rubric
	
	Total taking test: 29
	
	Total taking test: 29
	
	Total taking test: 26
	
	Total taking test: 26
		4 3 2 1
		Drawing Conclusions
		    (12) (5) (10) (2)
		Cause and Effect
		    (13) (6) (8) (2)
		Inferences
		    (10) (8) (5) (3)
		Sequence
		    (12) (7) (5) (2)			

Table 7-2. Cumulative Scoring Records for Final Student Product

FINAL STUDENT PRODUCT	SCORING TOOL	TOTALS BY CLASSROOM			
		4	**3**	**2**	**1**
Poster Project Students were given a list of criteria in which to make a poster to show what they know about the four reading skills (including two for the essential knowledge layer and five for complex-thinking layer).	Total taking test: 29 Total taking test: 29 Total taking test: 26 Total taking test: 26	Drawing Conclusions (15) (6) (7) (1) Cause and Effect (16) (5) (6) (2) Inferences (11) (7) (5) (3) Sequence (12) (7) (5) (2)			
Student Self-Assessment The team was aware that students should be encouraged to self-reflect and self-assess throughout the learning process. They used several templates for "during learning" assessments, but have chosen Strategies and Thinking Skills for the final student assessment, to give students the opportunity to reflect on their learning.	Ungraded—intended for student self-reflection and teacher feedback only	Drawing Conclusions (19) (6) (4) Cause and Effect (19) (7) (3) Inferences (15) (8) (3) Sequence (16) (7) (3)			
Oral Reading With Questions For the third time, teachers called back small groups of students to read passages. They asked students to demonstrate one or more of the four reading strategies as they read. Teachers prompted or asked questions if students continued to need help. The same checklist was used again to show progress in using these strategies.	Total taking test: 29 Total taking test: 29 Total taking test: 26 Total taking test: 26	Drawing Conclusions (16) (5) (7) (1) Cause and Effect (16) (4) (7) (2) Inferences (12) (10) (2) (2) Sequence (12) (7) (5) (2)			

In looking at overall content areas in which students showed low performance, the teachers wanted to know two things:

- How will we reteach these areas?

- What will we do with the students who have already learned it?

Because this unit assessment plan is ever-evolving and the teachers have an ongoing desire to achieve better results, they won't ever be satisfied that they are finished with the common assessments they have created. They know that in analyzing results, individual student performance is just as important as class performance. Considerable variations among students can indicate classwide weaknesses, demonstrating the need for changes in assessment-task components or in the overall format or structure of the common assessment, sequencing, or teaching methods. If a particular class is showing weaknesses on multiple assessments, the best strategy might involve seeking support and guidance from a mentor teacher regarding effective instructional and assessment strategies.

Through the creation, implementation, and results analysis, each teacher had the opportunity to learn about his or her own teaching strengths and weaknesses, areas that they would reteach, and assessments that need to be reworked and improved. Because students were involved in the process of focused assessment from the very beginning stages of learning, they were consistently informed as to their performance level with specific feedback and guidance for improvement.

Converting Scores Into Grades

Some districts have already designated methods for converting rubric scores into grades, so a teacher's first assignment would be to find out if there is a predetermined plan for this conversion. Some experts recommend making a direct transition from rubric points (4, 3, 2, 1) to grades (A,B,C,D). However, this is effective only if the performance criteria have been spelled out clearly and the goal or standard is broken down into subcategories, so that each component is assessed individually prior to the cumulative scoring. Other experts recommend converting rubric scores into percentages.

The fifth-grade team at Pleasantdale Elementary had created an overall rubric for the use of reading strategies, with each component of the standard broken down into separate goals. They decided that students' performance would be rated on each of those components. Their performance criteria and descriptors set a very clear target for each of the goals they wanted students to achieve.

The team had also created individual rubrics and other scoring guides for each of the activities within the unit. They would look at scores on the individual activities and compare those to the descriptors for the overall unit rubric as shown in Table

7-3. This would help them ensure that they were remaining as objective and true to the goals of the standard as possible.

Teachers and students need to discuss these expectations prior to the learning activities, so that all parties are focused on the goals and know what is expected. In addition, teachers should share the assessment design grid, in which they check off the exact activity formats for assessments in advance of the learning. Teachers might even demonstrate examples of what a "4" would look like by modeling a reading excerpt using the designated strategy. When the expectations are clear and students have had a lot of practice with specific feedback, then it would be fair to convert scores into grades or percentages. The Pleasantdale group decided that a 4 would translate into a grade of A, a 3 would be a B, a 2 would translate to a C, and a 1 would become a grade of D. Students who did not attempt the assignment would receive an F.

The teachers had agreed in advance that the oral reading with questions was the most indicative assessment of students' ability to effectively use reading strategies. This particular assessment allowed teachers to sit in small groups with students as they read orally and explained their strategy use. It also allowed for some differentiation, because some learners could be given a less difficult passage to read while still using the targeted reading strategies. Because this assessment task was given in both the growth assessment and final student product categories (Tables 7-4 and 7-5 on pages 168–69), teachers had two scores to add to the cumulative score. As a result, that assessment would be weighted more heavily in the final tally.

Table 7-3. Overall Unit Rubric

PERFORMANCE CRITERIA	EXEMPLARY 4	PROFICIENT 3	BASIC 2	NOVICE 1
Goal 1 Demonstrate the use of reading strategies to *draw conclusions* for reading comprehension of literary and expository text.	Independently draws conclusions with clear explanation and connections using evidence from the text and personal knowledge, ideas, or beliefs	With teacher prompts, draws conclusions with explanation using some evidence from the text and some personal knowledge or ideas	With guidance, draws some conclusions and shows a small amount of evidence from the text or personal knowledge	Attempts to draw conclusions without accuracy or demonstration of connections to evidence
Goal 2 Demonstrate the use of reading strategies to *determine cause and effect* for reading comprehension of literary and expository text.	Independently determines cause and effect with clear explanation and connections using evidence from the text and personal knowledge, ideas, or beliefs	With teacher prompts, determines cause and effect with explanation using some evidence from the text and some personal knowledge or ideas	With guidance, determines cause and effect and shows a small amount of evidence from the text or personal knowledge	Attempts to determine cause and effect without accuracy or demonstration of connections to evidence
Goal 3 Demonstrate the use of reading strategies to *make inferences* in reading comprehension of literary and expository text.	Independently makes predictions, interpretations, and inferences and clearly explains connections using evidence from the text and personal knowledge, ideas, or beliefs	With teacher prompts, makes some predictions, or inferences with partial explanations using the text and personal knowledge or ideas	With guidance, makes some inferences and shows a small amount of evidence from the text or personal knowledge	Attempts to make predictions or inferences without accuracy or demonstration of connections to evidence
Goal 4 Demonstrate the use of reading strategies to *sequence information* in reading comprehension of literary and expository text.	Independently recognizes and uses sequencing as a reading strategy and clearly explains connections using evidence from the text and personal knowledge, ideas, or beliefs	With teacher prompts, recognizes and uses sequencing as a reading strategy with partial explanations using the text and personal knowledge or ideas	With guidance, recognizes and uses sequencing in reading and shows a small amount of evidence from the text or personal knowledge	Attempts to use sequencing as a reading strategy without accuracy or demonstration of connections to evidence

Table 7-4. Student Name: Marcella Rodriquez

GROWTH ASSESSMENT	TOTALS BY INDIVIDUAL STUDENT	
Strategy Reminder List Students were given a strategy reminder list to use during the reading of a passage as they practiced the skills of drawing conclusions, cause and effect, making inferences, and sequencing. This was scored with a rubric and used as part of the cumulative score that will be translated into grades.	Drawing Conclusions	3
	Cause and Effect	3
	Inferences	2
	Sequence	4
Writing Prompt Teachers provided a prompt for all four strategies (two for the essential knowledge layer and five for the complex-thinking layer) and asked students to share their current understanding and example for each strategy. This was scored with a rubric.	Drawing Conclusions	3
	Cause and Effect	3
	Inferences	3
	Sequence	3
Textbook Assessment Students were asked to read a nonfiction selection from the text that required them to use the four reading strategies (two for the essential knowledge layer and five for the complex-thinking layer) and answer questions at the end of the selection. This was scored and compiled with other growth assessment scores.	Answer Key 94 = A	
Oral Reading Wth Questions This time when students read a passage orally and were prompted to share the reading strategies that they were using, the checklist was scored and compiled with the other growth assessment scores, as students received specific feedback and practice in this skill. The same checklist that was used in the preassessment was used again in order to observe student growth.	Drawing Conclusions	4
	Cause and Effect	4
	Inferences	3
	Sequence	4

Table 7-5. Student Name: Marcella Rodriquez

FINAL STUDENT PRODUCT	TOTALS BY INDIVIDUAL STUDENT	
Poster Project Students were given a list of criteria in which to make posters to show what they know about each of the four reading strategies (two for the essential knowledge layer and five for the complex-thinking layer).	Drawing Conclusions	4
	Cause and Effect	4
	Inferences	3
	Sequence	4
Student Self-Assessment The teachers were aware that students should be encouraged to self-reflect and self-assess throughout the learning process. They used several templates for "during learning" assessments, but have chosen Strategies/Thinking Skills for the final student assessment to give students the opportunity to reflect on their learning.	Drawing Conclusions	4
	Cause and Effect	4
	Inferences	4
	Sequence	4
Oral Reading With Questions For the third time, teachers called back small groups of students to read passages. They asked students to demonstrate one or more of the four reading strategies as they read. Teachers prompted or asked questions if students continued to need help. The same checklist was used again to show progress in using these strategies.	Drawing Conclusions	4
	Cause and Effect	4
	Inferences	3
	Sequence	4

The team practiced making the grade assignments with a sample of a few individual cumulative student records to ensure that they would be as consistent as possible. It was easy to see that Marcella Rodriquez's final grades taken from the growth and final student product assessments would average out to the grades shown in Table 7-6 (page 170). Ideally, it is best to place an emphasis on a student's most consistent level of achievement in arriving at a score, but that isn't always possible given time constraints. While not perfect, averaging scores does give teachers an overall picture of student proficiency.

However, before assigning these grades, teachers did go back to the overall unit rubric that they had created in order to review the standard and full expectations for the learning. Because Marcella was placed in the application layer of learning for this standard, she demonstrated (Table 7-6) that she has met the requirements of the expectations.

Table 7-6. Marcella Rodriquez's Final Grades

MARCELLA RODRIQUEZ	FINAL GRADE
Drawing Conclusions	4 = A
Cause and Effect	4 = A
Inferences	3 = B
Sequence	4 = A

As they reviewed final scores for students who worked in the essential knowledge layer of learning, teachers noted that these students were expected to become proficient only in two of the four reading strategies. These students need further teaching followed by further assessment. When assigning grades to students who were working in the complex-thinking layer of learning, teachers had to remember that the standard expected them to be able to use only four reading strategies for comprehension. Although these students were assessed on five strategies, in assigning grades, only the components that were part of the standard were factored in. The teachers will communicate the advanced efforts of these students in other ways—through notes on report cards, notations in students' portfolios or school records, and in student progress reports.

The Pleasantdale Elementary teachers have demonstrated one plan that meets their unique student needs, school protocol, and policies. This particular design for assessment unfolded as a result of dedicated teachers who were willing to engage in data analysis, exploration of better methods, discussions about what worked and what didn't work, and ways that the group could continually improve its efforts toward student academic success.

Final Thoughts

It's easy to get lost in the chase. Because the expectations in our profession are so vast, we tend to get caught up in the tangled details of teaching and assessing. But our primary objective at all times must remain student academic achievement. Student success is dependent on the teacher's knowledge of the subject, proficiency with engaging teaching practices, and consistent assessment of student understanding. This includes the creation of a plan for what to do when you see that some students aren't "getting it." Whether you create an assessment plan individually or choose to function as a collaborative team to create your plan, assessment must be continually planned, reviewed, and revised. It must guide your instruction and cause you to make changes based on the results you are seeing. It must be part of every lesson, every day.

So where do you start? Review the continuous learning cycle model on page 13 to be reminded of the four components of focused assessment: preassessment, informal assessment, growth assessment, and final student product. The cycle shows us that even as students reach the final student product, there is still much more learning to come. That ongoing learning may be a result of reteaching, connecting the current learning to future concepts, or periodically reviewing important concepts.

Lay the groundwork for assessment. First, who will be involved in the creation, implementation, and reflection of the assessment? You may be designing assessment on your own, but consider involving students as well. The more they are brought into the process of assessment, the more focused and engaged they will be throughout the instructional cycle. Students can become involved in the process by choosing assessment formats and creating some of the questions; they can also act as key players in communicating assessment results during parent-teacher-student conferences.

It is often helpful for teachers to come together in grade-level or content area groups, so that you have others with whom to share ideas, divide the workload, engage in research, and come to consensus about standards to be taught. This is also a time for discussion about the depth to which a content standard must be taught. Brainstorming with other professionals is a highly effective method for solving problems, sharing formats and strategies, and gaining new ideas.

As you lay the groundwork, review prior test data to determine the greatest needs of your students. In addition, check the components of local, state, and national assessments to determine learning targets that are weighted the most heavily—in other words, content areas where there are the most test questions. This provides a method for prioritizing unit assessments to create first. After you have determined the greatest need, analyze the content standards to ensure that you are clear about the breadth and depth that students are expected to master. Then spend some time developing the vocabulary that students will need to know in order to be successful with the assessment. These terms may come directly from the wording of the standard, or they may be words that are related to it.

Start working your way from learning targets to the creation of assessments. This entails looking at the standard, creating criteria, and developing either a performance assessment with a rubric or a selected-response assessment with an answer key.

Next, choose an assessment format or design that will be the most effective for the knowledge or skill that you will be teaching. Keep in mind that since focused assessment is about ongoing learning, it is best to use performance-based formats as much as possible.

Customize the assessment by creating three learning layers. All students will be expected to reach the level that the standard is calling for, but they may not all reach it at the same time. Create rubrics for all three layers with slight alterations.

Bring all of the components together by creating a unit assessment plan. To ensure that your formative assessment plan is using the continuous learning cycle, create assessments for each of the four categories: preassessment, informal assessment, growth assessment, and final student product.

Finally, launch the unit and reflect on your results. Ask yourself questions to determine which components could have been more effective and which had positive results. With student academic achievement in the forefront at all times, here are the two questions to concentrate on:

- What did the teacher learn about his or her teaching and student learning?

- What did the student learn about his or her own learning?

We'll end with some final tips that state the essence of *Focused Assessment: Enriching the Instructional Cycle.* A focused assessment is all of the following:

- A natural component of the instructional process—not a component that is tacked onto the end of a lesson

- A way to inform the teacher about how to make changes and modifications to the teaching activities and lessons

- A way to inform teachers about better ways to assess student learning

- A way to inform students about areas in which they are doing well and areas in which they need improvement—with specific teacher feedback

- Purposeful and meaningful to students

- Ongoing, coinciding with instruction

- Varied so that students with different learning styles have opportunities to demonstrate their understanding in ways that make sense to them

- A reflection of student data, content standards, and the information that was actually taught

Tools and Templates

The resource in this section can also be found at teachinginfocus.com.

Tool 31: Analyzing the Results

QUESTIONS TO PONDER	NOTES OR IDEAS
By individual student, what were the deficient areas related to? · Higher order questions · Certain content areas · Lack of reading/writing proficiency · Lack of cultural relevance · Emotional/social student situation	
In looking at common incorrect responses by individual classroom, answer the following: · Were students' incorrect responses consistent or varied? · Was the topic or content taught to a great enough depth in deficient areas?	
In looking at common incorrect responses on assessments, answer the following: · Were students' incorrect responses consistent or varied? · Were the assessment questions and directions worded clearly?	
Look at overall content areas in which students showed low performance and ask the following questions: · How will we reteach these areas? · What will we do with the students who have already learned it?	

References and Resources

Anderson, L., & Krathwohl, D. (2001). *The taxonomy for learning, teaching, and assessing.* New York: Addison Wesley Longman, Inc.

Authentic tasks. (2000). North Central Regional Educational Laboratory. Retrieved December 3, 2007, at www.ncrel.org/ sdrs/areas/issues/students/atrisk/at41k3.htm.

Baumann, J., & Kame'enui, E. J. (2003). *Vocabulary instruction: Research to practice.* New York: Guilford Press.

Black, P., Harrison, C., Lee, C., Marshall, B., & Wiliam, D. (2003). *Assessment for learning.* New York: Open University Press.

Black, P., & Wiliam, D. (1998). *Inside the black box: Raising standards through classroom assessment.* Retrieved December 3, 2007, at www.pdkintl.org/kappan/kbla9810.htm.

Boston, C. (2002). *The concept of formative assessment.* Retrieved December 3, 2007, at www.vtaide. com/ png/ERIC/Formative-Assessment.htm.

Boyd, V. (1992). *School context: Bridge or barrier to change?* Austin, TX: Southwest Educational Development Laboratory.

Brown, F. G. (1981). *Measuring classroom achievement.* New York: Holt, Rinehart & Winston.

Caine, R., & Caine, G. (1994). *Making connections: Teaching and the human brain.* Menlo Park, CA: Addison-Wesley.

Carr, J., & Harris, D. (2001). *Succeeding with standards: Linking curriculum, assessment, and action planning.* Alexandria, VA: Association for Supervision and Curriculum Development.

Chapman, C., & King, R. (2005). *Differentiated assessment strategies: One tool doesn't fit all.* Thousand Oaks, CA: Corwin Press.

Daneman, M. (1991). Individual differences in reading skills. In R. Barr, M. L. Kamil, P. Mosenthal, & P. D. Pearson (Eds.), *Handbook of reading research: Vol. 2* (pp. 512–538). White Plains, NY: Longman.

Donovan, M. S., Bransford, J. D., & Pellegrino, J. W. (Eds.). (1999). *How people learn: Bridging research and practice.* Washington, DC: National Academies Press.

DuFour, R., DuFour, R., & Eaker, R. (2007). *All things PLC.* Retrieved December 3, 2007, at allthingsplc.info/wordpress.

DuFour, R., DuFour, R., Eaker, R., & Karhanek, G. (2004). *Whatever it takes: How professional learning communities respond when kids don't learn.* Bloomington, IN: Solution Tree (formerly National Educational Service).

DuFour, R., DuFour, R., Eaker, R., & Many, T. (2006). *Learning by doing: A handbook for professional learning communities at work.* Bloomington, IN: Solution Tree.

Goodrich, A. H. (2000). Using rubrics to promote thinking and learning. *Educational Leadership, 57*(5), 2, 13–18.

Graves, M. F. (2002). Vocabulary instruction module developed for Reading Excellence Act.

Guskey, T., & Marzano, R. (2001). *Natural classroom assessment.* Thousand Oaks, CA: Corwin Press.

Hill, J., & Flynn, J. (2006). *Classroom instruction that works with English-language learners.* Alexandria, VA: Association for Supervision and Curriculum Development.

Hirsch, E. D. (2003). Reading comprehension requires knowledge—of words and the world: Scientific insights into the fourth-grade slump and the nation's stagnant comprehension scores. *American Educator, 27*(1), 10–48.

Hord, S. M. (1997). *Professional learning communities: Communities of continuous inquiry and improvement.* Austin, TX: Southwest Educational Development Laboratory.

Joyce, B., Weil, M., & Calhoun, E. (2000). *Models of teaching* (6th ed.). Boston: Allyn & Bacon.

Louis, K. S., & Kruse, S. D. (1995). *Professionalism and community: Perspectives on reforming urban schools.* Thousand Oaks, CA: Corwin Press.

Marzano, R. J., Kendall, J. S., & Gaddy, B. B. (1999). *Essential knowledge: The debate over what American students should know.* Aurora, CO: McREL Institute.

Marzano, R., Pickering, D., & Pollock, J. (2001). *Classroom instruction that works.* Alexandria, VA: Association for Supervision and Curriculum Development.

Mayo, C. R., & Shotts, C. T. (May/June 2004). Test results: Creating a road map for NCLB. *Principal, 83*(5), 22–25.

Senge, P., et al. (1994). *The fifth discipline fieldbook: Strategies and tools for building a learning organization.* New York: Doubleday.

Smith, J., Smith, L., & De Lisi, R. (2001). *Natural classroom assessment.* Thousand Oaks, CA: Corwin Press.

Sousa, D. (2001). *How the brain learns.* Thousand Oaks, CA: Corwin Press.

Stahl, S. A., & Fairbanks, M. M. (1986). The effects of vocabulary instruction: A model-based meta-analysis. *Review of Educational Research, 56*(1), 72–110.

Stiggins, R. (2005). *Student-involved assessment for learning.* Englewood Cliffs, NJ: Prentice Hall.

Sylwester, R. (1995). *A celebration of neurons.* Alexandria, VA: Association for Supervision and Curriculum Development.

Tomlinson, C. (1999). *The differentiated classroom: Responding to the needs of all learners.* Alexandria, VA: Association for Supervision and Curriculum Development.

Ahead of the Curve: The Power of Assessment to Transform Teaching and Learning
Douglas Reeves, Editor
Learn the ideas, insights, and proven strategies of the most influential luminaries on assessment in this compelling anthology.   **BKF232**

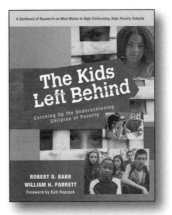

The Kids Left Behind: Catching Up the Underachieving Children of Poverty
Robert D. Barr and William H. Parrett
Successfully reach and teach underachieving children of poverty with the help of this comprehensive resource.   **BKF216**

Total Instructional Alignment: From Standards to Student Success
Lisa Carter
Replace an antiquated education system with a flexible, proactive one that ensures learning for all by focusing on three important domains of the alignment process.   **BKF222**

Whatever It Takes: How Professional Learning Communities Respond When Kids Don't Learn
Richard DuFour, Rebecca DuFour, Robert Eaker, and Gayle Karhanek
Elementary, middle, and high-school case studies illustrate how professional learning communities respond to students who aren't learning despite their teachers' best efforts.   **BKF174**